Is Anybody Out There?

By Rachel Pallitan

To
Sean,

I hope you enjoy reading
my life story as written
so far!

Rachel

ISBN: 978-1-304-12888-1

This book is printed by LULU (on demand printing)

www.lulu.com/pallitan

Dedication

I dedicate this book to:

Jesus Christ who loved me enough to rescue me from a dreadful and hopeless existence and to my brothers and sisters who I love and cherish. Though our lives were shattered and we did not form normal relationships we have remained a remarkably close knit family despite it all.

Prologue

Picking up the pieces of a broken life is not easy and some never recover. I hope this book will help some people to overcome by the release of pain and for others to have a better understanding about how to handle the lives of those who are so broken they cannot function correctly in society.

Disclaimer

I would like you to enjoy this book without feeling that I am intending to want revenge on or judge any person. My aim is to give insight into victim's lives and, at least, how the consequences of my past caused damage to my once happy personality. How my behaviour changed for the worse. How I malfunctioned in society and the way I chose to get the help I needed in order to make my road to recovery; though much of that does not come in this book but in its sequel.

All names and places have been changed and some entirely fictional to protect the identities of individuals who were and still are involved in my life and for legal reasons. It is not about the names and places but about the subject of my life; abuse of children and often abuse of adults who were abused as children.

This book is written chronologically so any questions the reader may have could well be answered later on either in this edition or its sequel.

I have meticulously corrected any mistakes in formatting and spelling to the best of my ability so if you do discover any at all and I hope none, please overlook them and forgive me. Thank you.

NB Words in italics represent my thoughts except when in brackets.

Introduction

My father was born the first son and fifth child to Bernard and Sarah Pallitan, in India on 10th November, 1923. He was brought up in St Catherine's Catholic orphanage in Debbingford, Kent which was run by the Sisters of Charity. His parents came back to England where his father died. The smoke of the East Indian Railway, where he worked as a guard and possibly other factors caused the lung disease. He was not, however, a smoker. My father was only five years old at the time. When old enough he ran away to join the Royal Navy and served his country for twelve years and had reached Petty Officer Status. When his contract with the Navy ended, after he married, he left in order to make a family life; my mother had insisted on it when he was about to extend his service and go on another mission to Korea. He already had two sons and was away at sea while my mother stayed at home to bring them up.

My mother was the first child of the Reverend Charles William Plowder and Agnes his wife. She was born on her mother's birthday 28th March, 1927, at home in Halwent, Yorkshire. What more perfect a gift than a baby to arrive on your special day? Her father was a Primitive Methodist Minister. She is now a vague memory to me. The impact of her death rippled throughout my life. She had given birth to six children; three boys and three girls. Her fatal accident unleashed my father against his children. Someone we had not been familiar with emerged from within him; not the man who walked on his hands round the kitchen with money falling out of his pockets, causing inspiration and admiration. The cruelty of his life was about to spill over onto his descendants. None of us were spared his tongue, hand or foot.

At age nineteen, as a consequence of those early years, I suffered a nervous breakdown. Internally, I was disjointed and perplexed, full of anxiety and fear. My circumstances, through lack of guidance and love, led me on the journey you are about to read.

Contents

Chapter One

Early Years

As I was not yet five years old I started at St Augustine's Roman Catholic Primary school in Trinton, Kent, two weeks after anybody else in my class. I walked quietly two hours late into the classroom with my mother. She asked the teacher where to sit me and led me to my place. After sitting on my chair I heard her talking to the teacher for a long time. I did not see her leave, she had not said goodbye.

At my table with four other children I rocked my little chair backwards and forwards. The movements were gentle at first and then much harder. If somebody did not notice me I would wet myself. I did not know how to ask the teacher for the toilet and she ignored me for ten minutes. My wooden chair scraped backwards loudly across the floor in little jumps until Miss woke up as I almost bumped into her desk.

'Theresa, take Rachel to the toilet, will you?

'Yes, Miss.'

Theresa stood up from sitting beside me and took my hand. Feeling embarrassed I followed her out. We walked through another class full of older children learning their times tables. We passed the head master's office and crossed the empty playground into the toilets with yellow speckled walls. They smelled musty. Stale air hung all around me and I did not want to breathe any more. My hand hurt as I touched the sharp grey specks sticking out from the pale paint.

Settling down to school life was difficult at first but I soon got to enjoy all the new things we did not have at home. The first book I loved to read was Janet and John. My teacher always encouraged me when I read at her desk.

At eleven o'clock every morning we looked forward to our third sized bottles of milk. The silver tops showed a little white straw peeping through the middle. I drank the freezing cold milk with relish. A tiny drop left at the bottom invited us to make it disappear. The attempts we made to have the cleanest bottle sounded like a hundred carts grinding fine gravel. I soon found the best way to do it.

'You have to drink slowly not leaving any bubbles behind,' I told Paul who was sitting next to me.

I could make my bottle look as clear as crystal.

After our break the teachers brought out tins of crayons from a cupboard. The special red boxes had 'oxo' written on in white. I knew what oxo cubes were but had never seen a box as big as that. I searched the untidy crayons for my favourite colour, orange. Well, that day it was orange; next it would be pink or yellow. I drew our house with Mummy and Scamp, our dog, in the garden. We did not have an apple tree at home but in my picture one stood proudly on the page with its red apples. I chose new crayons with the wrapping crisp and unspoilt, leaving the old stubby ones alone. Miss Newcombe proudly looked over my shoulder and said,

'That's a good drawing, Rachel.'

I looked forward happily to my beef dripping sandwiches at lunch time. Their taste reminded me of my mother walking about the kitchen. She had to leave all the fat that dripped from the meat of the Sunday roast in the roasting pan to set and change to an off white colour overnight. If she did not it would be too runny for the sandwiches. It was only called dripping when it had set. In my mouth it had the texture of fine, damp icing sugar but nowhere near as sweet and sometimes a bit of brown jelly shocked my taste buds. Other times I had marmite which bit my tongue and did not fill me up.

Sometimes, when my brothers took me home from school, a note was stuck on the front door. That happened quite a lot. Alan, my eldest brother, read it, 'Dear Alan, when you come home get dinner ready. Peel the potatoes; put peas in the saucepan and the sausages under the grill. I'll be home later on. Love, Mummy.' He removed the note from the door as a sign that he was home. Mummy was at work. I always wanted a note written out especially for me. Alan always got them and I thought Mummy had forgotten about me or did not like me.

A few weeks later I was able to walk the long way home by myself. At three o'clock I made my way out through the school gates and crossed the road. I looked back at the black school railings. The big, grey climbing bars, a centrepiece in the playground, were empty. Children who climbed on them at playtimes were not there anymore. The highest bar in the middle was for the older children to swing from right way up by their hands or upside down with the backs of their legs hooked over. Some girls did not swing upside down because their dresses or skirts flopped towards the ground covering their heads and showing their underwear; it did not matter because they were just children. The left hand bar attached to it was for the slightly younger ones and the smallest bar attached at the right, for us infants. At first I was scared to use them. Some children cut their heads open as they fell off. I was careful and never did that. It was raining hard so I took my mac *(raincoat)* off and held it over my head. I turned back and looked straight ahead at the white railway gates with a big, red circle in the middle.

Usually before a train was due we watched closely at the man walking around in his signal box. We could see clearly because the lower part was made of brick and the upper part had a lot of big windows all around it. It stood on the opposite right hand side at the edge of the gates. Richard had told me to watch the man pull the levers and then turn a great big handle around. I do not know why the man pulled the levers but as he turned the huge handle the gates closed slowly. The big, red half circles met in the middle making a whole one. No cars or people could cross. Everybody stood perfectly still, only lifting an arm to wave at the passengers, until the dark green train slowly passed by. It had just left Trinton station. Sometimes when the gates closed we ventured over the bridge and watched the train go underneath us. That day I was alone. There was no train coming but I was scared to walk across the railway lines because of all the rain pouring down. I managed to reach the next road but the rain was getting heavier and I could not go on anymore. I looked right, left and right again but the rain was like a car that never stopped coming. There was no room for me to cross. I stood and waited hoping it would stop but it never did. Just then a man came from nowhere and picked me up, he carried me to his milk float across the road in front of the dairy depot.

'Where do you live?' he asked.

'171 Mill Lane, Blackbridge, Trinton, Kent.'

He set off without another word and drove slowly along a road I did not know. A little later we arrived at my house. The kind man lifted me out of his float, walked before me up the garden path and knocked on our blue front door. Mummy opened it.

'I picked up your daughter,' said the man, 'she was trying to cross the road but it was raining so hard that I brought her home.'

Mummy said thank you to the man, closed the door and turned to me,

'I told you never to talk to strangers.'

I could not understand her. I had not spoken to him except to answer his question and he had brought me home safe and sound. Mummy gave me a present even though it was not my birthday and it was not wrapped. She told me to trace the pictures of my new activity books. I knelt beside the couch with the books on the seat. One had a picture, then a piece of tracing paper, then a picture and another piece of tracing paper and so on. I loved the dot to dot pictures most. The other small book had invisible pictures. I had to scribble over the pages in pencil to reveal what the pictures were. My mother did not come in with me but went instead into the kitchen. The loneliness was tangible and I felt forlorn on my own. Perhaps Peggy and Samantha were asleep. My brothers, who got out of school later than me, were probably still in class or had just left to come home.

Having Mummy at home was a treat and I loved her. At the weekend she cooked the dinner. After preparing the cabbage she handed William, Peggy and me a raw stalk. Samantha was too young and did not have the teeth to chew one. Next she pulled out a huge, creamy coloured bowl from the larder and put sugar and margarine in together. With a wooden spoon she beat the two together until they were pale yellow and fluffy. I did not want her to spoil it.

'Can I eat it just like that? When I grow up I want to make it and eat it all without making it into cakes.'

She scraped out the bowl leaving the bits that cling to the side for us to clean off with teaspoons. Like little locusts we cleared it in seconds.

After the cooking and dinner she went out to clean St Felix Church on Witley Road, about twenty minutes walk away. Daddy was at home. I missed Mummy.

'Rachel, come here,' Daddy called. I walked into the front room where he was sitting on the rough armchair at the far end, next to the piano. The photo album lay open on his lap. 'Have you been looking at these?'

'No,' I answered truthfully.

'Pull your tummy in. Stand up straight. You did look at them, didn't you?'

'No.'

'How old are you?'

'Five.'

'Well, you should be ashamed of yourself. Tell the truth, have you been looking at them?'

'No.'

I began to squirm inside.

I did not understand why he was asking me. I glanced behind me at the open front room door and saw the outer front door was open. Daddy did not believe me and I knew things would not get any better. He kept on pestering me about the photo album and I kept looking at the front door. I thought of Mummy at the church and quickly planned my escape. If the door had been closed I would have no way out, being too small to reach the handle even on tiptoes. My determination to escape grew but I was scared to run. Daddy asked one more time,

'It was you, wasn't it? Pull your tummy in, stand up straight!'

I tried to straighten my shoulders but when I pulled my tummy in it would not flatten because of having my appendix out when I was four. I looked at the front door again and that time my head would not turn back to look at him. My legs carried me as fast as they could out of the front room, through the front door and up the lane. I heard Daddy behind me shouting at William, who was a year and a bit older than me, to run and stop me. I did not stop in the chase even though my shoe laces were undone. I turned around, William had given up. I made it up the first part of the lane and then with all my effort up the longer part to the top. On our part of the lane there were trees on the opposite side but on the upper part houses were on both sides. I had to stop to do up my shoe laces but did not know how so when I saw a lady walking towards me, I begged,

'Excuse me, please could you do my shoe laces up?'

She bent down and tied them up. I said a quick thank you and ran on. At the top of the lane I turned left along Witley Road, not stopping until I reached the church which was across the road. Standing opposite I safely waited until Mummy came out.

At home many times, as on that day, I dug my teeth into my bottom lip. The taste of salty blood continued over many months. The scabs never healed because of the continual habit.

October came around and as Catholics we had to say the rosary. Mummy set up the statues of Jesus, Mary and Joseph on a small table in the front room. Just before bedtime she lit the tall, white candles on either side of the colourful statues. We were ushered into our places and knelt down one behind the other. In front were Daddy and Mummy, behind them; Alan, then Richard, William, Me, Peggy but Samantha was too young and already asleep in her cot upstairs. We clasped the rosary beads in our hands. Daddy made the sign of the cross saying,

'In the name of the Father and of the Son and of the Holy Ghost,' he kissed the small crucifix that hung from his black rosary beads. 'The Sorrowful Mysteries,' he announced as he led us in prayer.

My fingers reached for the first bead. All together we uttered off by heart but without much feeling,

'Our Father who art in Heaven…', until the Lord's Prayer was finished.

After that we recited three Hail Marys and a Glory Be. My knees, resting on the thin carpet, became flatter by the second. I reached the next part of the rosary beads. This time we said an Our Father, ten Hail Marys and a Glory Be. God would not have been happy if we had missed even one Hail Mary. We did that five more times until all the beads were used up. Every October was the same. It was always dark outside so Mummy had closed the curtains and put the light on. When the candles were lit Daddy turned off the light and we continued in the soft glow from the small hot flames. My knees became numb and at last we could stand up. I rubbed them to try to get some feeling back.

Peggy and I turned to say goodnight to our parents and brothers, kissed them on the cheek and went to bed.

Just before bonfire night I had the mumps so had to stay in bed. I could hear everyone in the back garden so climbed out of bed in the dark and pulled the curtain away from the windows to look out. While watching Mummy giving sparklers to my brothers and Peggy I longed to be outside with them. I did not like sparklers anyway. Last year Mummy lit the end of a rope for me and showed me how to whizz it around in circles which made the end turn red but it did not catch on fire. I felt safer with that. She had made jacket potatoes by the fire and treacle toffee. I watched as Alan took a sparkler from Mummy, walk down the path and I knew where he was coming with it. Sure enough he came upstairs, into my bedroom and tried to give it to me and, though I loved my brother, I wanted Mummy to give it to me.

'Here's a sparkler. Mummy told me to give it to you.'

'I don't want it.'

'Here you are, just hold it.'

'I can't there's sparks everywhere.'

I was scared of all the sparks flying around and though I did not tell my brother I really did want to hold it. I watched as the sparks flew and the black used up end become longer, I desperately wanted to take hold of it before it went out but could not. *Mummy doesn't love me.* I watched the sparkler go out. It was too late for me to enjoy at all. I felt sorry for Alan and was confused about everything. Why did I have to have the mumps?

Another night I could not sleep because of an earache and, not being allowed out of bed, I started to sing monotonously,

'Mar…my, Mum, Mar…my, Mum, I've got an earache,' slowly moving my head from side to side on the pillow. No one came upstairs. My screams and hopes for a rescue were all in vain. The television was too loud and the door shut, blocking out my cries. 'Mar…my, Mum, Mar…my, Mum, I've got an earache,' I sang a little louder. Still nobody answered and my earache grew worse. 'Mar…my, Mum, Mar…my, Mum, I've got an earache,' I shouted even louder but still was not heard. My desperate cry grew with every breath. As it was not loud enough, from the very bottom of my lungs and the highest note from my throat, I

14

screamed, 'Mar…my, Mum, Mar…my, Mum, I've got an earache!' My shouts were at last acknowledged and I heard someone's footsteps coming up the stairs. Richard walked into my bedroom and I wondered why Mummy had not.

'Mummy has sent me upstairs to get you. You can come down.'

He reached up to the top bunk, grasped me with his nine year old arms then carried me downstairs to my mother's waiting lap. I sat gazing at her sewing bag on the table. The dark pink, silk base was embroidered with black flowers. It shimmered and contrasted with the black matt rim around the top. Cotton wool, safety pins and other things lay next to it together with a grey sock and a big smooth wooden mushroom. Mummy used to put the mushroom inside the sock to locate and spread out any holes so she could sew them better.

'Put your head to the side.' I leaned my head towards my left shoulder with guidance from her hand and, as she squeezed a black rubber thing from a bottle, I felt the cool drops flowing into my ear. There was a funny kind of crunching sound and then I went half deaf as she placed a cotton wool bung over my ear. 'That's it. Go up to bed now and get to sleep.'

Why didn't she cuddle me? Maybe it was because I should not have been down. I slipped off her lap with a heavy heart and went back to bed. My sisters were fast asleep. I put my thumb in my mouth, turned over and rocked backwards and forwards on my left side until the emptiness ushered me into a deep, lonely sleep.

Day passed into day and then one morning when I woke up, Mummy, Peggy and Samantha had vanished.

'Where's Mummy, Richard?' I asked when I next saw him.

'She's gone away. She's taken Peggy and Samantha with her. But if you tell anybody she will go to prison.'

'Oh.'

I tried to understand. Richard turned away and went downstairs. I followed after getting dressed and after breakfast was sent back to my room for doing something I should not have done. Daddy did not tell me what it was. Everything was quiet as I stared at the empty railway tracks outside my bedroom window. Mummy was somewhere on a train and I did not know when she would ever be home again. *Why didn't she take me too?* I had to stay in my bedroom until I was sorry for what I had done. *I am sorry now. I* thought I knew how sorry was supposed to look and feel like - ashamed with my head down. Walking downstairs slowly, and making sure I was thoroughly sorry, I found Daddy in the front room.

'I'm sorry, Daddy.'

'Don't do it again.'

'No, I won't.'

What did I do? Shrugging my shoulders slightly I walked away from him.

The following week at school during playtime I hardly played with the other children. Instead, I leaned against the wall thinking of Mummy and how I loved her.

'My Mummy will never die,' I said to my friends or anyone who came across my path.

Every day I leaned against the wall and told everybody the same thing. I did not want to play like the other children anymore.

There were no notes on the front door for Alan when I got home from school. I waited in the back garden for my brothers because they had a key to get in.

'When is Mummy coming home?' I asked Richard.

'I don't know. She might be coming home tomorrow and make sure you don't tell anyone she has gone away.'

I stared numbly into the emptiness.

Two weeks went by and Mummy had been away for so long when, as usual, I dawdled up the path coming home from school and there it was, the piece of white paper stuck to the door. *Mummy's home!* I read the note, 'Dear Alan, I have gone shopping. Peel the potatoes and put beans in the saucepan. The sausages are under the grill. I will cook them when I get back. Love, Mummy.'

Mummy was home again! Like a fairy she was rarely seen, but I knew she was working hard somewhere. When she was at home with us, magic filled the air. If I told her how happy I was she would go away again. That Saturday it was sunny and warm outside. Mummy was at home with us. While I was in the front room a man walked past the side window. *It's the man with the polish.* I rushed into the hall where Mummy opened the door to his knock. She bought a big tin of polish and three tiny ones.

After closing the door she gave me one of the small tins. Peggy and Samantha got one too as we all loved to help. As I returned to the front room with the others following me, tiny flecks of silver dust danced around in mid air as the wind blew through the open window.

'We've finished in here now. Let's go upstairs and do the bedrooms,' said Mummy.

We followed her upstairs where she swept all the 'dead people' out from under the beds. They had turned into grey fluff, snapping fast like a magnet to the broom. Mummy peeled them off with her hand and threw them away in the dustpan. She picked up the Humpty Dumpty rug and shook it out of the window then placed it neatly down on the lino, beside the bunk beds. Her yellow duster was covered in dust and fluff also, so again she shook off the dead people from that. They flew off into the air and away up to Heaven. The dead people from the duster were luckier than the ones who ended up in the dustpan because Mummy put those in the dustbin and put the lid on. They could not escape and had stuck together too thickly to be able to soar through the sky.

A few mornings later William was singing,

'Mar-my, Mum, Mar…my, Mum, can we get u… up?' in his bedroom.

When we heard him we joined in from ours with heads turning from side to side but Mummy did not answer for a long time. We knew she would when it was time to get up. When she did come she came into our room first, her hands laden with our freshly washed and ironed clothes. As she placed them on Peggy's bed, she said,

'We're going to the seaside today. Get dressed quickly, come and have breakfast, then we can go.'

'We're going to the seaside!' I squealed in excitement, jumping up and down. Nobody else seemed as excited.

'Put your bodices on.'

Bodices were my favourite clothes. The pattern down the front of the thick, white tops made them more special than plain vests. Our other clothes were hurriedly put on, buttons done up scewiff then Peggy and Samantha started to get excited too. Mummy dressed Samantha then brushed our hair and put a red ribbon in mine. She had already prepared the picnic basket so when everyone was ready; off we went to get the coach. As I climbed onto the first step I breathed in a sweet sandwich like smell, though it was not sandwiches but a distinct and special smell that I always smelt when we went on a coach.

After a wonderful day watching my brothers riding donkeys and enjoying making sand castles with buckets and spades, I sat on the coach in a seat on my own. Mummy was sitting on the other side, one seat back, where I could not see her and I had no idea where my sisters or brothers were sitting. I was so very tired and wondered whether I was allowed to lie down. I wanted to ask Mummy but she was busy chatting to the lady she was sitting beside and ignoring me so I could not ask her. I was afraid of getting into trouble but decided to lie down quietly and have a much needed nap. My tense body tried to relax but I did not sleep. A short time later I felt something being draped over me. Mummy just kind of threw it and was gone again. I felt lonely and vulnerable without her beside me.

Two days later I was in the kitchen alone after coming home from school. Our dining table was covered with a scarlet, velvet type cloth with tassels all around and on the top was a large cake. My eyes transfixed as I followed their line of attraction. I wondered what the white stuff was on the top and clambered onto a chair to have a closer look. I placed the forefinger of my right hand on top and watched it sink in slightly then took it away to find some of the wet, white mixture covering it. Quickly, I licked my finger and found it had the most delightful, sweet taste. *It must be there for us.* My finger had no time to think for itself. Immediately, it set back to work furrowing as far as it could go across the top of the cake. Long, straight lines resembling tracks in the snow were left behind as my finger leapt to my mouth until there was nothing but a bare cake. When Mummy came into the kitchen and noticed the difference, she exclaimed,

'Who's been eating the icing on the cake?'

Oh, wasn't I supposed to? I was unable to answer while trying to work out why she seemed upset. After all it was the first time I had ever seen something like that.

A couple of months later in December, just before Christmas, Mummy called from her bedroom,

'Rachel!'

I scrambled out of the shed where we are playing.

'Coming!'

'Come and listen outside our bedroom door but don't come in.' I crawled upstairs on my hands and feet and waited. 'Are you there?'

'Yes.'

'Listen with your ear to the bottom of the door and tell us if you can guess what it is.' I put my ear towards the narrow crack of light. 'Do you know what it is?'

'No,' too scared to say anything more. They tried again but I told them I could not tell what it was.

'Okay, go downstairs again.'

Early on Christmas Eve we were sent to bed for a sleep before getting up for Midnight Mass. It was cold when Mummy woke us to get dressed. One big family we walked into the dark of winter and shivered. Mummy and Daddy walked in front of me. Samantha held Mummy's hand; she looked cute wearing her pink coat, bonnet and muff. At two years old it was the first Christmas she walked to church. Peggy walked beside me holding my hand and the boys marched smartly behind us.

Christmas morning! The usual song was sung and we got up when answered. Daddy took us into the kitchen and pointed to the empty plate and glass on the table,

'Look, Father Christmas came last night, ate the mince pie and drank the sherry and the reindeer has eaten the carrot. Let's go into the front room and see what he has left in there.'

The Christmas tree stood beautifully decorated in the corner. A table supporting the tree was wrapped around with Christmas paper, like a curtain, to prevent us looking underneath at the presents hiding there. The light from the window brought a bright shine to the baubles hanging on the tree.

'Sit down, everybody,' instructed Daddy.

We sat down round the room in order of age. Daddy put his hand inside the 'curtain' and pulled out a present. He read out the tag and handed a gift to Samantha. She opened it with some scrambling help from Alan, Richard and William. After we watched Samantha open her present to see what she had got Daddy pulled out another present and read the tag. He gave it to the child it was for and, as with Samantha, we all waited until it was opened. That was the way we got our presents until they were all opened. There were some from Aunty Jean and Aunty Monica then Mummy went out of the room and upstairs. We all waited for her to return. She carried a huge present into the front room and read the tag,

'To Rachel, from Father Christmas.'

Wow, what a big present! I knew what it was, a walky talky doll. I knew it upstairs when I was listening at the door but did not want to say or I would spoil the surprise. I just knew it was because of the talking. It was not long before the wrapper was off and my doll free. Samantha and Peggy were nearly the same size as her.

'She's got fair hair.'

Mummy stood her on her feet, held her shoulders and then let go.

'She's standing on her own,' I said, surprised.

I don't deserve this doll. I looked at Mummy and turned my gaze to fix it for a second on Daddy wondering why I got it. He came over and put his hands on the doll's shoulders. She put one leg in front of the other and walked across the front room with his help. Her little white shoes would fit Samantha. *I will try them on her later when no one is watching.* Mummy unzipped the doll's flower patterned dress. Her back had what looked like a right angled nail sticking out of it. Mummy grasped the 'nail' with her fingers and turned it round and round and at the same time the doll sang,

'Baa, baa, black sheep, have you any wool?'

I was delighted. Everybody loved my doll and wanted to play with her. As long as the nail was turned around she sang nursery rhymes.

'What is her name going to be, Rachel?' asked Mummy.

I thought of all the girls in my class who I liked the best and decided,

'Julie.'

'Julie is a nice name.'

'No, I want to call her Carol.' And Carol she was.

'I have still got *this* present.'

I ran upstairs to get my favourite book. Mummy had given it to me when I was four but I could only look at the pictures then. Daddy waited for me to come down and then continued to give out presents. I left my book on the table. William got some marbles and dinky toys, so did Richard and Alan. I liked to play with those too. Our presents got all mixed up as everybody was playing with everybody else's, sharing their excitement. I got a plastic tea set and a sweet shop with lots of miniature cardboard packets full of sweets and things which I shared out on the tiny plates. Mummy had left the room to get dinner ready.

After dinner at the dining table in the kitchen and having asked if I could get down, I wandered back into the front room; we were not allowed in if the door was closed. I picked up my book and turned to my favourite page; the one with Away in a Manger written in it. I read out loud with all my heart the last verse, which I loved the most:

'Be near me, Lord, Jesus
I ask You to stay
Close by me forever
And love me I pray
Bless all the dear children
In Thy tender care
And fit us for Heaven
To live with Thee there.'

I thought of all the children in the whole world, gathered them in my heart and lifted them up towards Heaven as the verse became a sincere prayer.

A little later, Daddy called to Alan.

'Alan, come into the shed.'

'Coming.'

That was where Daddy kept his workbench, across the hall opposite the front room. We were all waiting outside the shed while Alan and my parents went in. Daddy had carried a gigantic present in there. Alan was allowed to go in and open it.

Afterwards Daddy opened the door and we were all allowed in.

'Ooh, a slide.' Richard gasped.

Our breath was taken away as we stared in wonder. In order of age we queued up at the bottom of the slide steps. We had to be careful not to break it or fall off. Somebody stood guard at the bottom. One day during a storm I was going down the slide when the black electricity meter box cover flew off the wall just as I reached the floor and hit me on the head. It was not a serious injury, only a lump, but it baffled me for a while and I slowly went to tell Mummy, who was cleaning upstairs, what happened. She came down immediately and noticed a hole in the wall. Our house had been struck by lightening. No more playing in there after that for one day.

My sisters and I enjoyed rare occasions when Mummy was at home with us. We played sometimes in the bathroom where Carol sat on the stool and did the splits. Peggy and I could not make her sit properly, making us squeal with laughter.

'Stop that giggling,' Mummy shouted from downstairs.

Our laughter only increased. The more we laughed the more Mummy repeated herself but she never came up to see what we were doing. I never could work out whether she was angry or not.

One evening when Mummy came back from work she asked Alan,

'What is your favourite colour?'

'Black.'

Then she asked all of us in turn; Richard chose red, William chose yellow. Of all colours I chose grey because it was different and I was sure nobody else would choose it. It would have been the rejected one. I did not think she would find a grey whatever it was she was asking for. Nobody questioned my choice. Peggy chose yellow and Samantha black. The following day Mummy brought in a whole lot of dishes with handles either side, tea plates, dinner plates, cups and saucers. We had one set each. Two had black and two yellow so which was whose out of who chose them did not really matter. I was pleased with my grey colour.

Mummy took me to Mass with her at times. On one occasion I was restless and fidgeting, she told me to be still many times but to no avail, until she whispered in my ear,

'Jesus will be coming down the aisle in a minute.'

'When? When is He coming?'

'In a minute, shh.'

Jesus was coming down the aisle! I must not miss Him. He would be wearing a white robe. *I hope I see Him.*

'Where is Jesus, Mummy?' I asked whilst looking towards the back of the church.

She did not answer. I asked again and again making more noise then than before. At the end of Mass Jesus had still not appeared and I got nothing more out of my mother regarding seeing Him. The only really important Person had not turned up. He did not want to come. I could not believe that He had not come. The disappointment crushed my young heart. With my head hung down while walking home, still in sadness, I stared trancelike at my mother's feet. I noticed her shoes were pointed at the toes. How she fitted them into the tips of the high heels I could never fathom. I was sure her feet should have been pointed when she took her shoes off but they were completely normal. I had seen some women running in their high heels and never thought they could walk let alone run in them. Being under the impression that only children ran, I laughed, and especially when they ran in those shoes. *I will never wear high heels or pointed shoes when I grow up.*

We children played together many times. On a rainy day we found games to play indoors. One game was where Alan lay down at the bottom of the stairs. The rest of us, one at a time, went up a step and jumped down onto his tummy. He hardened his muscles tight so it would not hurt. We continued going up an extra step each time and jumping until he could not cope with the force of the jump anymore. After Alan, Richard had a go at lying down and then the rest of us in order of age. With Samantha we were careful as she was not as capable as us older ones to tighten her muscles.

On one of those days, at a time when we were having a break from the game, Daddy bent down towards me and said,

'I've got a headache.'

'Can I pray for Jesus to take it away?' and, with concern, lay my right hand across his huge forehead,

'Lord, Jesus, please take my Daddy's headache away. Has it gone?'

'Yes, it's gone.'

I could not have been happier than at that moment. I had never seen anyone do such a thing to anybody before but my spontaneous act and prayer, together with Daddy saying his headache had gone, led me to believe I was doing the right thing.

At six o'clock, my bedtime, when Samantha and Peggy were already in bed, I often looked down in fascination at Samantha's fair hair and freckle free face. William, Peggy and I had ginger hair and freckles. Samantha slept on her back with her arms bent at the elbow. Her hands rested either side of her head and her new, big teddy lay on the floor beside her bed. Sometimes I pinched her to make her cry. I could not quite work out why she cried when I pinched her arm as her mouth was not connected to it but she made the cutest sound. I was not aware that what I was doing hurt her and she could not talk then so could not tell me. When finished with that I climbed up the ladder to the top bunk, put my knees up, thumb in my mouth and closed my eyes.

Some weeks later, after waking earlier than usual one morning, I stood at the top of the stairs. I was not supposed to be awake so early but could hear Daddy talking to Mummy downstairs. I knew he would be taking her to work. Wanting to see her before she went but knowing I could not talk to her, I hid behind the wide pillar at the end of the banister and watched as he took her coat from the hook and held it open for her to put on. Listening to what they were saying I became concerned for her.

'I don't want you to go today.'

Daddy pulled her coat away again.

'I am going, I want to go.'

'I don't want you to go.'

Mummy reached out for her coat and he reluctantly helped her put it on. Mummy wanted to go. *Let her go if she wants to go.*

'I don't want you to go today. You are going to die if you go to work today.'

'I want to go.'

I did not understand but I did know Mummy wanted to go to work. *Let her go if she wants to go.*

Daddy opened the door and they left.

Chapter Two

Death of my mother

It was Thursday the 20th of April, only four days after Peggy's fifth birthday. Alan and Richard had done the chores they were supposed to do and we were all sitting in front of our nine inch, black and white television set watching the news. I did not like the news but it had to be on for when Daddy got home. I liked to see 'Watch with Mother' programmes such as Andy Pandy and The Flower Pot Men. All of us especially loved Torchy the Battery Boy and my brothers liked Rin Tin Tin. A train went by outside the window while we watched television, to which my brothers sang,

'Last Trai-een to San Fernando, last Trai-een to San Fernando, if you miss this one you'll never get another one, dooby, dooby, dum, dum, to San Fernando'.

I kept looking out of the window to see when Daddy brought Mummy home but they did not come. We sat quietly waiting because there was nothing else to do.

Oh, this is them. No it isn't.

'It's a policeman!'

As the sound of Richard's voice filled the room we all rushed to the front door in anticipation. Alan opened it, barely giving the policeman a chance to knock. Richard stood next to him. The rest of us gathered round. The policeman only stared at dark haired Alan, fair haired Richard, three little redheads and fair haired Samantha.

'There's been an accident,' he stated calmly and just walked away.

We went back to watching the television, not knowing what his announcement meant. At half past seven, when our parents were still not home, Alan took charge,

'You girls better go up to bed.'

'What altogether? Can't I stay up till Mummy comes home?'

I wanted to say good night.

'No, because it's half past seven already and you all better be in bed when they come home.'

In bed I waited for the sound of the front door opening. When I did hear it open, there were no voices. They must have gone straight into the front room and closed the door. I still could not hear any talking and was not allowed out of bed to see. After a long time and keeping my eyes closed because I was supposed to be asleep, I heard the front room door open. Somebody was coming upstairs. In the silence I dared not move. Even when Daddy put his finger next to my face I still did not move. He was wearing his cold leather motor scooter gloves. I wondered why he left his finger there for such a long time and without a word seemed to stand perfectly still. *He isn't breathing.* I waited with my eyes closed for him to go away. When I did dare to open them he had vanished but what was that? I reached out in the dark. It was not his finger but a packet of sweets! He left them there by my cheek. Putting them under my pillow I wondered if my sisters had got some as well. Everything remained very quiet and I fell asleep.

In the morning Daddy explained to us all in the kitchen that Mummy had gone to Australia and told me,

'Rachel, you are Mummy now.'

I knew I could not be Mummy to my brothers because they were older than me but to my sisters I would be a good mother. My childhood ended there at the young age of six and a half. My father's orders were that the eldest should take charge when he was not at home. Whoever that was must report to him the behaviour of the other children. As Mummy had trained all of us to some degree in housework it was easy to carry on. Alan did the shopping and Richard did the washing in our twin tub then squeezed the clothes flat through the attached rollers. My mesmerized eyes watched the clothes pass through as he turned the handle. Water oozed out at one end while the clothes that passed through the rollers became as flat as cardboard and almost dry. Daddy bought a spin dryer later which spun the clothes so fast that William and I pulled the unrecognisable clothes and sometimes sheets and pillowcases from around the edges of the drum and put them into a basket. On a fine day we hung the washing out on the washing line while standing on tiptoes. Our chores became endless; we also had the washing up to do and mostly I dried the dishes. Alan and Richard cooked most of our meals.

In the front room the knitting machine stayed untouched where a partially knitted garment hung from a long row of needles. Strands of different coloured wool lay across it. The silence of the hand machine's clatter spoke loudly about the departure of the person behind its activity. My father could use the machine and also knitted by hand with knitting needles, having learned it in the Navy. He left the machine idle for weeks before finishing the tank top my mother had started. Nobody touched it out of unspoken respect of her missing presence.

Some time later we were introduced to our twenty six year old cousin, Martina. She came down from London to look after us and the house; she was a gentle and quiet lady so I cannot remember her that well. She sat by our beds at night reading from a book but I would not listen. I wanted my mother and kept making deliberate noises until she left and went downstairs. We did get to love Martina though and after getting used to her gentle character we expected her to stay for a long time. Then one day she suddenly announced she was leaving which left us all stunned. We thought she liked us too but she was going. Our sadness took a long time to dislodge.

Next to come to look after us was Mrs Maisings. She was as old as Nanny, Daddy's mum and a real friend to me. William washed the dishes after meals and I dried them. Mrs Maisings sat opposite supervising in her grey clothes. As I dried the plates her magnetic presence drew me close to her like an invisible elastic band. The further I walked from her to the draining board the greater the tugging to return. Taking the smile and the sweet she offered, I smiled back,

'Thank you.'

When her time was up the most notorious of women took her place; Mini Twist. That troublesome woman took a lot of rebellion from all of us.

'Which one of you will go up the lane and find cigarette ends for me? Look, like this one. Don't get the ones without any white paper on and I don't want them with the brown tips at the end.'

She was a bully as well and we did not stand for it. She cooked cabbage till it turned brown and we had to eat it. Richard reported her to Daddy. Our frustration with her was short lived and she was soon packing her bags. Small faces peered in relief at her departure. *I hope she never comes back.*

After Mini, Maria came with her little son, Jake. Maria worked hard in the house while we played outside. She was the only one who did not expect us to work in the house. While playing with my sisters one morning I heard a knock at the kitchen window.

'Rachel, come here.'

Maria wants me, it must be levenses.

'Yes?' I answered nearing the back door.

'Don't stand on the fence.'

'Alright.'

I went back to play and, looking next door, stepped back into the thick 'diamonds' of the wire fence. I held onto a wooden stake and swung it backwards and forwards. I enjoyed the swinging, comforting movement until I heard another knock on the window, *Oh, oh*! Jumping off the fence I called,

'Samantha!' and put my arm round her shoulders then coaxed her, 'Maria wants you.'

When she left to see why, I jumped back on the fence.

'Tell Rachel to get off the fence.'

'You have to get off the fence.'

No sooner had I been told, I was up again, Maria knocked once more on the window.

'Samantha, Maria wants you,' I coaxed her a second time.

'No, she doesn't, she wants you.'

'No, she wants you,' I repeated.

'No, she's looking at you, see. Go and see what she wants.'

'No, you have to go,' knowing I was in big trouble.

'Rachel!' shouted Maria.

Oh dear, she does want me. After that second and final telling off I stayed away from the fence.

Staying out of trouble was hard for me. Maria's son Jake was my age and I always managed to make him cry, though whatever I had done was hardly worth crying about. I had to think of something fast to make him laugh so he would forget about it.

They did not stay long and Maria was the last home help outside of the family.

Nanny was due to arrive shortly after Maria left. On the afternoon of her arrival I skipped and ran towards home on my return from school to a waiting Nanny standing in the middle of the front garden path with her hand hovering above her eyes, shielding them from the sun like Mummy used to.

'Hello, Nanny, hello, Nanny,' I greeted her with a wide smile.

'Get upstairs and tidy your bedroom!' she shouted in reply.

I turned instantly into cardboard. *Isn't she pleased to see me?*

I treated all adults in that hearty way. As I skipped to school I said hello and made unhappy looking adults smile. My golden, wavy hair flew on the air current of their returning smiles. I loved everyone in my class and did my best to concentrate on the lessons and especially enjoyed spelling tests because I mostly got them right.

I never looked forward to going home to Nanny though. One night when messing about I could not settle down so was told to go downstairs and sleep with her in the front room. She slept on the couch which turned into a double bed when pulled down. I dreaded the thought. She wore a hair net which made her look funny and very different. I was glad I did not have to wear one. She kept her teeth under the bunk beds in our bedroom in case we got up in the night.

'If you get out of bed my teeth will come after you,' she warned.

To know that her teeth were under the bed with all the dead people as dust was not very pleasant. During the day she said the bogey man would be hiding in a cupboard and if we were naughty he would come out and get us or we would be put in there. I made sure never to open a cupboard or be naughty. The thought of a bogey man was really scary because he was not a good character. I could not even imagine what he looked like. I only had visions of the dark inside of the cupboard and vanishing into it if he ever got hold of me. I lay in bed with Nanny, thankfully minus her teeth which I knew were guarding my sisters. She turned on her side and faced the piano. I had a little bit of bed but preferred not to be there at all. I thought if I was to move and she found out she would tell me off so very slowly, an inch at a time, I edged towards the mattress ridge. There, I made my rolling off escape but was quickly caught half way down by the sagging blankets. As I could not help myself get back up I slept cradled there until morning. When Nanny left we did not have any more people to look after us.

The previous routine for our household re-emerged. We faithfully carried out our chores but sometimes Daddy summoned our attention with,

'Alan, get everybody down to the kitchen and line them up.'

He was angry. Like little soldiers we scrambled to face him. Our arms hung neatly by our sides whilst we stood to attention in order of age. He continued,

'Right, who did not bring the milk in from the doorstep this morning?' Nobody answered as we fearfully prepared for what was coming next.

'Alan, was it you?' he demanded of my eleven year old brother.

'No, Daddy.'

'Hold out your hand!'

Alan held out his hand and got a hard smack. On down the row he asked the same question. Each answer was, 'No, Daddy.' Each of us got a less severe smack than the previous one but still it was enough to hurt. My father would have none of it and insisted,

'Who is the culprit? You are not going anywhere till one of you admits that they did not bring it in.'

He was extremely patient in matters like that. Each of us waited nervously for another to respond.

'I'll take the blame,' Richard finally and bravely offered.

'I'll take the blame.' was the usual response for the sake of the others. The one who took the blame was not necessarily the guilty one. My father was not happy with the admission but it prevented the situation from getting any worse. Richard received his punishment and we were free to get on with our day.

At night when Peggy coughed sometimes Daddy came in without a word. I was listening though like a little radar and heard the angry words he spoke in her ears,

'Stop it. Shut up,' he growled in a deep voice.

She could not stop it. He did not give her any medicine, just a vicious word that never took the cough away and so we slept in fear on those occasions.

Preparing for my first Holy Communion for a few weeks before the big Saturday event in June was not an easy task for a seven year old. I had learned to say confession to the priest so on the day before taking the host for the first time, recited to perfection,

'Bless me Father for I have sinned, this is my first confession; I have been telling lies and been disobedient to my parents and stole a penny out of Mummy's purse.'

Without the confession of sins, whether they were real or not, we could not take Communion. That confession was standard for me for two years even though the crime of taking the penny happened long before our mother died. The following day Daddy woke me at half past seven in the morning,

'Have a wash and clean your teeth.'

Eating and drinking was not permitted for three hours before Communion. All the other children slept and I felt Mummy's absence keenly. I slipped off the top bunk, had a quick wash then placed my wet, pink toothbrush on top of the bar of Sunlight soap pushing it forwards and backwards to make lather and scrubbed my teeth clean with the horrible tasting foam. After washing and dressing I met Daddy at the bottom of the stairs. He crouched down and handed me a carrier bag,

'Take this to school and give it to your teacher. She will put the dress on you.'

I took the bag and looked inside. There was no veil. While carrying the bag alone to the bus stop so early in the morning and on that special day, I felt empty inside. My birthday was on the same day as Our Lady of Seven Sorrows and because of that I reasoned that I was somehow special and had to suffer seven major sorrows in my life before I would not suffer anymore. My legs were not quite long enough to climb onto the step of the bus easily so I knelt and grabbed the vertical bar to pull myself on properly as the bus moved off. When I arrived at school the playground was empty. It seemed a long way to the classroom where I found my teacher waiting. We took out the white dress which had nothing fancy about it. She told me to stand on the table so she could make sure the hem looked straight. Just the two of us and the isolated atmosphere hung like a heavy morning fog.

'You haven't got a veil?'

'No,' I answered flatly.

'Well, never mind.'

Eventually the other girls arrived wearing their beautiful dresses and veils. The boys looked smart in their short, dark grey trousers, white shirts and blue sashes. Their mothers and some fathers were with them. Silently, I joined all the children as we formed a line in twos in the playground to march round to the church next door. Our Lady of Trinton was a dark church. I had been baptised there when only ten days old. We had to be baptised because if we were not we would not go to Heaven if we died before we knew right from wrong. The sooner we were baptised the better.

'It's cold in here,' I whispered to Sylvia who also did not have a veil.

We marched down the aisle and knelt in the places we had been given in a previous practice. Sylvia vomited and was taken out. The colourless stone statues embedded into the wall facing us, behind the altar, looked foreboding. I did not like it in that church as much as the more modern one on Witley Road. The Mass was slow and it was a long time until the altar boy closed the railings so that we could kneel in front of them. It was a holy moment and we would be holding Jesus' body in our mouths. Because I had been to confession I felt accepted by God and when the priest came to me with the host he held it up in reverence for a second or two before announcing,

'The Body of Christ.'

'Amen,' I replied.

I stuck out my tongue for him to place the host on top. Once it was there I was careful not to crush Jesus. He stuck fast to the upper part of my mouth and that was a problem. How was I to swallow Him? Should I leave Him there until He was dissolved or was I allowed to peel Him off with my tongue? I was not sure what to do so left Him where He was. On that day only we were allowed to have Communion wine straight afterwards so that helped moisten Him a little. If I moved my tongue I wondered if anybody would notice my mouth moving and that would spell lots of trouble and my first Communion might even have been made void. Nobody had told us what the texture was like and what huge problems we would face. I still had not swallowed

Him when I left the church and we were not allowed to open our mouths with Him in there as that was considered sacrilege. I just had to let Him slowly dissolve and remain silent until He was completely gone. I did worry when bits broke off and I swallowed them. Was Jesus hurt when He tore like that?

After the service we famished children were taken back to the school where breakfast was served. I sat at the side of the classroom entirely alone watching the others with their parents; how proud they were of their children. Nobody helped me to anything but there was a lump in my throat which came of its own accord as if to say, 'Don't worry, I'll stay with you forever.' It would not go away.

Not many days afterwards and Peggy had been at the school for a year, she and I arrived early one morning. I walked into the playground but Peggy was somewhere behind. The morning was in confusion and I saw a boy who was in my brother William's class walking across the playground at a fast pace. He was crying and his face bright red. I turned and looked all around me but could make no sense of the situation. When I saw Peggy I asked,

'What's the matter with Wallace Blaycot?'

'Harry has just been run over by a lorry outside the sweet shop. I saw his blood being washed away down the drain.'

She was crying and I stood in bewilderment. *How could he have been run over?* Again I looked around but could see nothing. There was no sign of a lorry or anything unusual that I could pinpoint an accident had happened but Harry was not in school that day, nor anymore. He was in Peggy's class and only six years old. I thought he was a lovely, well behaved, quiet little boy with the face of an angel. Both Peggy and I loved him a lot. Wallace, Harry's brother, had disappeared but when I saw him again I said how sorry I was for him. Harry had just bought an orange flavoured Jubbly from the freezer in the shop opposite and was walking over to the school when the lorry hit him and crushed his head. The whole playground froze in grief.

At home, as we became more confident looking after ourselves, some of our time was spent on outings to Happy Hill at the top of the lane. We loved to roly poly down the neat, steep, grassy slope. William always rolled straight but I curled towards the side and stopped half way down which was always disappointing. Our cardigans and jumpers collected dry grass as we rolled which had to be removed before we got home, to hide the evidence. Going to the swings was another favourite and was a long walk, even though only round one corner. Samantha sat in the baby swings with the wooden slats all around to make sure she did not fall out. When the three of us girls wanted the seesaw Peggy and Samantha sat together at one end and I, at the other end, sat lopsided enough so that one foot remained on the ground. I pushed the ground away and soared upwards then landed hard causing Samantha and Peggy's legs and bottoms to fly into the air. I could see the sky between them and the seat; that was known as the bumps. Samantha sometimes wanted to have a seesaw while Peggy was doing something else. On those occasions she almost always bumped far too high and jerked head first over the handles either falling off or banging her head on the opposite side. No matter how gently I pushed I misjudged her extra light weight almost every time. Other days Alan organised single file walking trips down the lane to the orchards or Waterside Creek. In order of age, with Alan leading, we trekked on the edge of the narrow, tree lined lane. First we had to pass under the railway bridge. If a train was coming I could not go. Why I was so afraid of the noise was beyond anybody's reasoning. My brothers and sisters looked forward to the approaching thunder of the wheels. I could not understand them either. Once under and beyond the bridge a lorry or car approached now and then in the opposite direction. There was only room for one car or lorry at any given time.

'Single file!' shouted our leader; to get us as close to the green verge as possible and out of danger. The ten or twenty minute walk to the orchards seemed an eternity. We passed apple, pear and plum orchards to get to a gravel footpath. A cherry orchard on the right was my favourite. Just the word 'cherry' brought the most heavenly sensation to what was sometimes a tedious walk. Opposite the cherries were more apples and in the autumn bright purple damsons, which were green inside, hung over fences for us to pick freely. Their sour taste, if picked too early was not divine, though the unique plum textured fruit, when ripe, was quite pleasing except for the stone which refused to come free from the flesh so often.

Occasionally, William led us girls to the orchards himself.

'You stand at the gate and if you see anybody coming start whistling at the top of your voice,' he instructed.

'Alright.'

Peggy stood beside me as William climbed over the fence and disappeared into the mass of trees. We stood perfectly still, only looking left and right. Minutes and what seemed like hours passed by. When a couple of older girls walked towards us we were on full alert so we started to whistle hard. The closer they came the harder we blew until they walked past. Danger over! Neither of us had worked out that they could hear us. On his return the inner and outer pockets of his jacket and his trouser pockets were bulging, not to mention his hands and mouth.

'Oh, look at your pockets! Can we have a cherry?'

'Well, only one. Here you are.'

The plump cherry rewarded my whistling lips with its sweetness. Its flavour, as I expected, could be compared with nothing else on earth.

'Can we have another one?'

'No, you'll have to get your own.'

'But how, my legs aren't long enough and Peggy can't.'

That was it for one day. On the way back up the lane towards home a lorry crept up behind us. William ran and jumped into the greenery to avoid being knocked down,

'They're stinging nettles!' he screamed.

Peggy and I kept as close to the curb as possible and stood still till the lorry passed. William quickly grabbed some dock leaves that were always growing nearby and rubbed the raised, painfully itchy patches on his skin with those which helped heal them before we arrived home.

Further down from the orchards was Waterside Creek and William took me down there with him on occasions. The tide was normally out. Strong smelling seaweed punched at us as we trudged along. Two tall, round, black, shiny towers stood erect awaiting our approach. William warned me,

'They're dungeons and if you go in a giant will come and shut you in. You won't be able to get out ever again.'

I peered all around and far into the distance; nobody was in sight so I relaxed but I knew the giant had long legs and could reach me fast. A gnawing horror lay sleepily in my stomach. William caught a crab and put it in the bucket he had taken from our garden. I was scared of those nasty things because of their pincers but my brothers did not care. They could never pick up the transparent jellyfish though which, when lying flat on the pebbles or sand, had what I thought were four eyes right in the middle, besides, they could sting so were left well alone. I looked out over the tideless wasteland and towards the old rusty ships that never went anywhere. One had a door in its side and I wondered how anybody got in or out as there was no handle. Craggy rocks and narrow paths often turned our shoes sideways as we clambered along the coast. To leave that place did not come easy but leave we had to.

Other times we took a much longer walk to Prickly Woods which was in the opposite direction to Waterside Creek. On our first visit Richard warned me,

'There's a bull and if you are wearing a red skirt it will chase you.'

I was wearing a red skirt. He showed me the sign which read, 'Beware of the bull.' I did not see the bull but was terrified in case it ran out of nowhere and hurled me into the air. *What if I never come down again?* The Woods were mostly grass and very steep with lots of bushes towards the bottom. We could not roll down without being afraid of getting caught in the thickets. The further we rolled down, the denser they were but the top part was flat and that is where we ate a picnic sometimes. There were lots of trees behind the flat part and it is there where the bull would suddenly come out and chase anything red but it never did.

Back at school day passed into day and at dinner times the infant classes were transformed into three dining rooms for the occasion. Dinner ladies stood behind their huge pots of food and next to them different coloured plates were piled high. I always wanted a pink one so counted them first and then counted the children in the queue to see if I would get one. We lined up at the tables to be served and then took our dinner to our seats. Salad was never my favourite meal as it was cold. Particularly on the plate was an odd, horrible tasting pea. I did not know its variety and feel sure they have been banned from the general public ever since. I chased it around trying to hide it and reporting its awful presence to a teacher did not help because nothing was to be left uneaten.

Sometimes there were too many children to have dinner in our school. From junior one the teachers picked the best behaved children who put their hands up to go to another school down the road. Once chosen, the lucky ones marched in twos quite a long way towards the sea and then turned left up to the other school. When I was allowed to go I noticed a gigantic, pale blue, rusty gas container at the bottom of the road before we turned the corner and wondered how the workers got gas into and out of it. If there were no rooms in it why were there steps up the side? I never asked anybody so did not find out.

Our days at home were interspersed with invitation cards for check ups at the dentist. We ignored them, too scared to let the dentist touch our teeth. There were other times when I had to go to the optician. At the appointment, while sitting in the waiting room at the clinic, a lady stood watching us. I looked up at her wondering when she would call my name,

'Stop looking over your glasses,' she glared.

I wondered why because she was looking over hers. Shortly afterwards I heard my name,

'Rachel Pallitan!'

I almost cried, not wanting to be there at all. No one in my class had to wear glasses. The nurse put drops in my eyes making my sight blurred. Next she put a flesh coloured patch, a bit like a plaster, on the right lens but I could barely see from my left eye with that on so when we arrived home after school I 'lost' them with William's help. He threw them into the blackberry bushes, without me seeing where, to prevent me from ever finding them. I wonder if anybody ever found them. If not perhaps they are still there. From that appointment William decided I was a perfect alibi to get out of school. Almost every week he came into my class, walked straight up to the teacher's desk and told her,

'Rachel has got an appointment with the clinic and I have to take her.'

With her permission I left my desk to follow my brother to a sweet shop nowhere near the school. On our way we walked along the pavement looking for used chewing gum. Not the dirty trampled into the concrete stuff. We only wanted the cleanest and best; bright pink or orange and hardly chewed. We could blow bubbles with that and it still tasted sweet. Once at the sweet shop I watched as William helped himself to all kinds of sweets and chocolates then followed him outside where he sat on a bench, unwrapped his goodies and ate them. Watching William eating his plunder, so often, began to affect my behaviour.

'Please can I have some, William?'

'No, you have to get your own.'

I decided it was the only way I would get a taste. Next time at the sweet shop William vanished and I hovered by the high counter. In my naivety I slowly reached up towards the nearest packet of sweets and picked it up. Immediately, the assistant shouted,

'Quick, ring the bell and phone the police.'

She stayed where she was while another went somewhere else. William arrived, grabbed me and we scarpered outside, hair on end. A policeman marched determinedly down the high street and I warned William,

'He is coming for us.'

'No, he isn't.'

So why was he looming up in our direction? He had not noticed us so we dodged quickly out of sight and, to get away fast, jumped on the next bus back to school. At the end of that and any school day my class sat in silence for at least five minutes before we were let out.

'Rachel! Rachel! Rachel!' My brothers and sisters shouted from the playground loud enough for all the school to hear.

My head swivelled towards the teacher but he took no notice. Not until we had our full five minutes silence did he let us out. I wondered if they would go home without me but thankfully that never happened. Once out, Richard and William led the way up the road. After passing the railway crossing they took a detour left towards Trinton football ground to show us where it was. We peered in to see as much of it as we could through the closed gates and about turned the way we came. Turning left we crossed the road up to the grocer shop on the corner.

'Have you got any specs?' my brothers asked the shop keeper.

We were given rotten apples, pears and anything else he could not sell. Some tasted like perished rubber but not as chewy, thank goodness. Many times when we visited the shop my sisters and I topsy turveyed over the bar outside while we waited for our brothers. Only one of us could have a go at a time. I put my hands on the bar, lifted myself onto it, leaned forward and swung into a somersault. As my feet left the ground I felt as free as a bird flying through the clear, crisp air until I landed back on my feet with a bump. The sense of soaring freedom lasted only a couple of seconds but was enough for me to know what it felt like to fly. At night times I often dreamt I could float in the air. My body lifted off the floor automatically and I hovered just under the ceiling. Sometimes it was scary because I did not know how to get down. Other times I dreamt I was on my yellow scooter, scooting up Mill Lane but instead of the wheels being on the pavement they floated about two inches off the ground and sped up the lane. Sometimes I did not have a scooter at all, it was just my legs. I did not even have to walk, my feet glided along at many miles an hour. In the dreams I never told my brothers and sisters what I could do. It felt like I had to keep it a secret. Other times, when going home from school, we followed our two brothers up a bit further to the baker's shop. Richard or William had found it. Once inside they asked the lady behind the counter,

'Have you any spare cakes?'

The smell of freshly baked bread and cakes was strong enough to keep us hungry for a week. I could not breathe it in long enough. They were given cakes and good ones too. Not stale like the specs that were off. We had to chew round the 'rubber' bits on the specs but my brothers and sometimes we girls ate a whole delicious cake. There was one drawback to our having things to eat on the way home from school though; our breath would give us away and that meant trouble with our father.

'Does my breath smell like I've been eating something?' the first to remember the punishment asked.

Our mouths opened for the others to take a sniff. If the answer was yes we would have to get rid of it by breathing out hard, lapping underneath our tongues to make saliva and swallow a few times before we asked to be checked again. Once we were all cleared it was okay to go home but there was no loitering. If we were late that would be another opportunity for trouble.

One day a small packet of biscuits went missing from a cupboard in the kitchen. Daddy sent Alan upstairs to call me down for questioning,

'Did you take a small packet of biscuits from that cupboard?'

'No.'

'If you own up I'll only give you two smacks.'

'No, I didn't take them.'

'Are you sure? You did, didn't you!'

'No, I didn't.'

'Right, you are not going to own up so you will get a good hiding.'

He then punished me severely. I cried from the pain and the injustice of his not believing my innocence. Two weeks later when he and Alan were clearing out the cupboard Daddy found the biscuits but I had had the hiding. He *gave* me the biscuits to compensate.

When my brothers made cakes and left them on the side my sisters and I sneaked a hand over the dresser and grabbed one then hid behind the long, plum coloured curtains which hung in front of the back door to keep the draught out. We munched away until Richard came and, noticing our shoes beneath the curtains, caught us. It was good fun being caught by him because he always made us laugh but we were not aware that it was not really a laughing matter when we were finally thrashed. Despite the trouble my brothers played with us many times. As we lay on the kitchen floor they held a hand above our tummies and waggled their fingers. Slowly they came closer and closer before suddenly tickling us. I laughed from the minute they waggled their fingers way above me and, as they approached, my laughter grew until finally reaching a crescendo,

'I wanna go toilet, wanna go toilet, wanna go toilet.'

Often that stopped the torturous play. Meanwhile, William wanted to see what made Carol sing so pulled the middle of her back out.

'Now you've broken it,' I said.

'It's a small black record.'

'You have to put it back so she can sing again.'

He could not, it was broken and Carol sang no more. The small nail in her back used to turn the needle in the grooves; from then on Carol had a big hole there.

Early one evening the three of us sisters were in the kitchen. While I was drying the dishes Peggy stood beside me with tempting words,

'Do you want a spoonful of sugar?' offering me a spoon to bite from.

'No.'

'Oh, go on, have one.'

'No, I don't want it, we're not allowed.'

Peggy persisted and I insisted no countless times. She fed Samantha, who too eagerly ate the forbidden sweetness. Peggy again tempted me and I was so fed up with it that I resigned angrily,

'Oh, alright then,' and snapped my mouth hurriedly round the entire bowl of the spoon hiding every trace of sugar.

No sooner had I given in when we heard footsteps coming down the stairs.

'Lick yer lips, lick yer lips' we desperately urged Samantha.

Not understanding why we pressurised her she remained sitting calmly innocent on the floor. Her lips covered in tiny sugar grains betrayed her sisters into the hands of another great punishment.

'What are you doing?'

'Nothing,' we answered Richard.

It did not take him long to notice the crystals nestling on Samantha's lips.

'Right, I'm telling Daddy.'

Nooo....

Richard disappeared back upstairs only to return with,

'Samantha, go upstairs, Daddy wants you.'

Sugar lipped Samantha toddled off upstairs and on her return she was crying. I quizzed her,

'What happened?'

'I got two smacks.'

Richard then summoned Peggy. On her return I enquired,

'What did Daddy do to you?'

'I got four smacks.'

She too was crying. *That means I'll get six.*

'Rachel, go upstairs, Daddy wants you next.'

In fear but confident in my six smacks I went to face Daddy. On arrival in my bedroom where Daddy was waiting, he demanded,

'Bend over the bed!'

I obeyed immediately. My father hit me, one, 'Sorry Daddy,' I offered, two 'sorry Daddy', three, 'sorry Daddy', four, five, 'sorry Daddy' six times. *That's six, I can get up now.* No, seven, eight, nine I counted and then lost count. I thought he was never going to stop and in desperation cried,

'I want to go to the toilet!'

Then he let me go. My confused mind could not fathom why I had been given such a severe punishment. I had done nothing wrong. In fact I had said no all the time to Peggy but all my doing right did not count. The following Sunday morning after Mass the six of us children sat round the dining table in the kitchen, as was our custom. The entire day was holy and no playing was allowed. Daddy stood behind us ironing the clothes. My back was towards him. Richard sat opposite William who was on my left and Alan sat opposite me; their faces expressionless. Peggy was at one end and Samantha at the other. Daddy, in anger, told everyone of all the wrong I had done and every now and then a hefty hand cuffed the back of my head. My world collapsed and I knew Daddy was no longer my friend. Humiliation crept into my bones and emptiness, even of my brothers' and sisters' presence, filled the air. Nobody was allowed to speak. My blue Sunday dress did not help. Its hem hung through the hole at the back of the chair. My hands rested between my legs forcing the front of my dress to touch the seat. Fear and dread swept over me as I needed the toilet. I knew if I was to ask to go Daddy would hit me again on the way out. Remaining silent was not the wisest thing to do. The time came when I could no longer hold on and, looking down, horror crossed my face. My dress had a large, darker blue patch right there in front.

'I want to go to the toilet,' I announced too late.

Covering my dress with my hands I went out. Daddy did not lift a finger as I feared. Once upstairs I quickly rummaged through the chest of drawers and found my pink plastic apron which I pulled out and tied around my waist. Not needing the toilet anymore I still went because if Daddy did not hear the chain pull more trouble would come upon me. Feeling silly with my apron on and nervous for the time when Daddy would ask me why I was wearing it, I approached the top of the stairs. The silent doom broke when I heard,

'Rachel, do you want to come to see Mummy's grave?' Alan's voice rose upstairs.

Fear tangled its fingers tighter around my heart.

'Yes.'

'Well, take your apron off then,' Alan said cheerfully as I reached the bottom of the stairs.

Oh no. I did not want to be suspicious about it so very slowly, knowing I would be in for another hiding, I untied the apron. After all I had only just put it on. Pulling it away from my waist I glanced down towards the threat. My dress was completely dry! *Mummy must be looking down on me.*

Without entering the kitchen again Alan and I left for the cemetery. We walked in single file along the worn footpath because of stinging nettles on either side. The railway line stood above us to our right and I stared for a moment at its stones while pondering the mass of electricity that could strike at the touch of a foot on the tracks. I felt safe walking behind my brother. The freedom of getting away from my father caused me to love Alan more. After half an hour we entered the gates of the cemetery and walked the long, wide paths, passing many graves on either side, to the very top. Alan filled one of the metal watering cans from a tap that stuck out of the ground on the corner just before we reached Mummy's grave. I helped carry the watering can. She was buried at the back of the cemetery without a headstone but her grave was marked with a number etched on a metal label – 502; the short grass gave no indication that somebody had been placed below it. No grave could be walked on out of respect and to prevent the dead souls being disturbed. Alan placed flowers in a vase and poured water in. We knelt beside the grave and prayed the Lord's Prayer, three Hail Marys and a Glory Be, then left for home.

Every Sunday was the same; they were Daddy's bad temper days. Every week after Mass when we came home he shouted angrily. He almost threw the hoover downstairs on one occasion as he took his frustration out on us. We stayed silent and still until the storm subsided.

Some days of the week, when not at school, could be quite pleasant as on the warm sunny afternoon when Richard started to dig a hole, the shape of a boat, in our back garden. Daddy put down the sieve he was shaking something from and helped Richard, with the rest of us, dig out the soil. Lots of tiny hands patted the seats until they were hard and flat. Our feet rested on the floor of the boat as though sitting on a bench. We covered the seats with old newspapers and sat inside ready to sail away. Richard made hats by folding newspaper which, when finished, looked like sailing boats themselves. Daddy did not get in the boat with us but kept busy pulling the heavy garden roller to flatten the soil on the rest of the garden before sowing grass seeds. He then prodded it with a garden fork but I did not know why. We were not allowed to walk on the soil for a fortnight where new grass would grow. When it did come, lots of chatter went on about the soft little green spikes peeping through the brown earth. After helping us and finishing what he was doing in the back garden, Daddy went round to the front garden to plant flowers. When we disembarked from the boat Alan had the idea to dig to Australia. He and Richard knew that to dig there they must first dig through the soil then, explained Richard,

'After we have dug out all the soil we come to water. When the water is all dug out we come to fire, when all the fire is dug out we come to Australia.'

I knew that would take a long time and my brothers did not take the matter seriously enough to even start. I stepped back into the boat, my sisters followed.

'Do you know why we moved here?' Richard asked me while removing his hat.

'No.'

'Because our garden collapsed where we lived before and made a great big hole. I nearly fell into it.'

'What, as deep as these boats?'

'No, I could have fallen in and not been able to get out.'

44

Just then the sound of an approaching train made us look towards the railway line. We waved at the passengers while watching the green locomotive pass by on its way to Blackbridge. Some people waved back. Then a plane flew overhead. My sisters and I, waving and calling, leapt to shore and in a chorus shouted to the pilot,

'Come down! Come down!'

I wanted it to land in our garden and let us fly with them. It never did but I thought maybe the pilot wondered if we were telling the plane to calm down.

If we ever reached Australia we would find our mother but I knew we had to find Scamp, our dog, as well because Daddy told us he was looking for her. As Australia was too hard to reach I decided Scamp might be nearer. Every day I called our dog. Our mother's return was possible and I never stopped searching for her. I recalled dreaming of the night she came to see me. My excitement grew as I saw her approaching but my siblings were not so ecstatic. Not understanding their calmness I made the best of my welcome to her and she explained early on that,

'I can only see you every Wednesday night but must be back in my grave by midnight or it will close.'

I kept the secret alive when I woke up and waited for the following Wednesday night but my mother never showed up. Disappointed, I resumed calling for Scamp. He was the only thing left to connect me with her. I snapped out of my night time memory and watched the boys make bows and arrows out of wood and string. We had great fun with those and when it was my turn to play I pulled the string with the arrow's chipped end snugly fitting the string until the tip of the arrow quivered at the centre of the bow. Aiming at nothing in particular and, sure my arrow would fly the furthest, I let go but it fell flat down to earth as soon as it left the string. My brothers' skill, however, gave the arrow good height and flight.

'I like it better here in this house 'cos of the trains and the bridge,' said William, looking over his shoulder.

'And we've got blackberries all along the fence,' I joined in as he let go of an arrow.

Stepping closer to the blackberries to pick his arrow up he reminded me,

'Yes, well you mustn't eat the green or the red ones or they give you tummy ache.'

'Well, I've had my appendix out when I was four and nearly died when it burst,' I declared.

'That's for eating a whole apple core with the pips in. You should never eat the pips.'

There was more to do in our garden besides all that; we collected pea bugs *(wood lice)* of all colours and sizes in a metal bucket. Some curled into balls when we picked them up and put them in the bucket. They rolled around just like peas. Others crawled onto our hands and tickled as they walked about. Richard arrived on the scene stating,

'And you let Billy our budgie out of the cage when you were four as well. He flew away and never came back.'

'That wasn't me.'

'Yes, it was, you left his cage door open.'

Despite the few happier days Daddy continued with his bad temper as on one Saturday afternoon when William and I played in the front room. The two barred electric fire mesmerised us. William found some silver paper which we rolled into a pencil shape and I placed it on the red hot bar to see if it would burn.

'It won't burn.'

'Well, keep trying then,' said William.

'Well, it has to burn.'

William took the paper off me and rubbed it up and down the bar till sparks flew, causing us to jump backwards. The bar turned back to its normal colour of grey but only on the part that sparked, the rest stayed red. We had broken it.

'Shh,' said William, 'what's that smell?'

'Bad eggs!'

Alan approached from the kitchen to investigate the strong odour.

'What's going on?'

'Nothing,' both William and I chimed.

'Yes, there is.'

He ventured closer.

It was no use we had to let him in to see. Daddy would surely find out but not yet as he was at work. Evening came and I was in bed when Alan came to tell me to come down.

'Did you do this?' Daddy snapped.

'Well, it was me and William.'

'Go and get William!'

I left my father and, feeling relieved that I may not get the punishment this time, I climbed the stairs with my stomach churning.

'William!' I shook him. 'William, Daddy wants you.' I shook him again. 'William, you have to come down.'

No matter how hard I shook him he did not wake up. I went down again empty handed and told Daddy William would not wake up. That was the end of it. Although I was baffled as to why Daddy had been lenient, I knew William was not really asleep. I was glad for him not to be punished. However, next day, which was Saturday, Daddy was still very cross. I stood before him in the front room and without warning he kicked me hard so that I landed underneath the chair just inside the door; like a football being kicked into the goals. I stared at him from there wondering if something else would come my way. I did not know that it was wrong to be treated that way. Daytimes became much of a battle ground, not safe at all and bedtimes for me were quite a lonely experience, especially when nightmares were present. One I had was of a big grizzly bear chasing me. In the dream I ran and hid behind my father's back, he did nothing to protect me. I told him there was a bear but he carried on sitting unperturbed

There were no trips to the seaside with Daddy. Fun times were absent in his presence and when it came to haircuts there were no hairdressers except him. He owned a pair of hair cutting clippers and often skinned my brothers' heads to stubble. The low crunching sound of hair passing through the blades as Daddy squeezed the steel handles together and out again for so long almost sent us to sleep. He used to perm Mummy's hair. She looked funny in her translucent, pink, ultra thin curlers as we called them. The unforgettable smell of the solution filled the kitchen and cleared any lurking debris from our lungs. Daddy took out small, thin, oblong bits of paper and wrapped strands of Mummy's hair in them and then applied the curler, closing its clip firmly in place but he used a bowl on Samantha's head so she looked like a monk when he finished. After Daddy cut

Richard's hair one day he told him to go and get my summer dress.

'Put it on,' he commanded.

For him it was a joke and as we watched Richard put it on, Daddy laughed. Richard did not but stood for all to see in the kitchen and was glad when Daddy said he could take it off. My best summer dress with pale flowers dotted about all over it and straps at the shoulders seemed ruined all at once, like Daddy hated it. Richard was a boy and he felt silly. I do not know what Richard thought of Daddy. Perhaps Daddy wanted to know what Richard would look like as a girl but he did not look anything like one, even wearing that.

On Sundays and Holy Days such as Christmas, Easter and various saints' days, we continued to go to church where my three brothers served as altar boys. After Mass we collected the hymn books and put them away at the back of the church. William, when Daddy did not come with us, showed us how to help ourselves from the open collection plate on the table which was also at the back.

'Look, you do it like this.'

He put his hand on the collection coins and took a penny or two. Where a space was left he moved other coins to close the gap. I managed to get a penny sometimes. We ran to the Freep's shop across the road and bought chews, liquorice or black jacks which were our favourite. Outside the green grocer part of the shop *(adjacent to the sweet shop)* there were all sorts of things. I loved especially the multicoloured dog biscuits in the huge open sacks. It was easy to take one or two because nobody stood guard. On days when the shop was closed we sat on the front step, on the sweet side, until Mr or Mrs Freep put some chews through the letter box for us. Sometimes they invited us to play with Micky and Susan in the garden at the back. They had toys that we did not have so it was always a treat. In our garden Daddy gave me a newspaper to play with but did not tell us how so I put it on my lap and turned the pages to look at the pictures or see if there was anything we could colour in. Peggy and Samantha stood by me as I shared what I could of it. Sometimes we were allowed scissors and cut out shapes to look through.

On one sunny Sunday morning when Daddy came to church with us we passed the Freep's shop on the way back and while walking beside me he explained,

'When I was a little girl I wanted to put nail varnish on.'

So I thought that because he was a little girl when he was younger and was now a man that I would be a man when I grew up and that my brothers would be ladies but never voiced my thoughts because of my childlike trust in everything he said. Then he walked faster and kept telling me to hurry up but my legs ached while trying to keep up with him. After dinner during some of those afternoons at home he asked me to lie on the bed with him. He went to sleep while I lay on the far side of the double bed. Afraid of waking him up, in case he made me stay, I silently sneaked head and arms first over the edge of my side and slipped onto the floor. On my hands and knees I crawled past the window and out of the room, fearful of being caught. On another occasion he asked me to get into the bath with him,

'Only if I can have my swimming costume on and you put your trunks on.'

He did put his trunks on but I felt awkward in there with him. He appeared relaxed and harmless but something inside me was on alert. It did not feel right and did not happen a second time.

Because we were so conscious of our behaviour and having been taught to report back to Daddy we were also conscious of God and His punishments. If any of us misbehaved and another saw it we sternly reminded each other,

'God's watching you.'

It brought a fear of our Creator. We were not taught much about His love. So how and why did I look so forward to seeing Jesus in church that Sunday when Mummy told me He was going to come down the aisle?

Richard and William took me round the side of our church on Witley Road after Mass one Sunday where Richard pointed down some steep steps and towards huge black windows,

'You see in there?'

'Yes.'

'That's hell. Behind the black there's loads of fire. That is hell and that's where you go when you commit the mortal sin.'

I was not quite sure what the mortal sin was but thought it was blasphemy. I stared, trying to see a glimmer of the hot orange flames but the black windows were too solid. Hell was so horrible that we were not allowed to see in there.

'I don't want to go down there.'

To be burned beneath the church without hope of getting out ever again was too much of a nasty thought.

Summer and autumn finally gave way to winter and another Christmas Eve. William shouted to me from the bedroom,

'I just saw Father Christmas on his sleigh.'

I ran upstairs as fast as I could to see him, panting,

'Where?'

'He's gone now.'

'Where did he go?'

'Go to the other window and you might see him.'

I frantically searched the skies but he was nowhere in sight; no reindeer, sleigh, red suit, presents or anything else! I knew William had seen him and I should have been watching with him instead of doing other things. Christmas Day was similar to last year except, of course, for our mother's absence.

New Year came and went then one dark evening the following February I was in the bath with my sisters just before bed. Peggy and Samantha stood at the 'blunt' end and I stood at the tap end in shallow, cold water. We had no running hot water so Richard brought up boiling water from the kettle and while pouring it from the steaming spout, instructed,

'Rachel, go up to that end.'

'No, I can't,' being afraid of the boiling water coming from the spout.

Richard continued pouring, swung the kettle towards me to warm up my end and the scalding water gushed over my legs. I screamed until he quickly slapped me hard across the face which brought immediate silence. I had seen it in films where hysterical women were slapped bringing the same outcome. We had to be quiet because of Daddy. He was downstairs and that spelled danger.

'Tell Daddy I can't come down to say goodnight,' I told my sisters. 'Tell him I've got a headache.'

I went to bed after Richard put a cream coloured bandage on my stinging legs. In the morning I let out another scream as I saw huge blisters the size of tennis balls protruding from between the sparse dressing and my red skin. I showed Richard, who in turn ordered William,

'Go and phone the doctor from the phone box. Tell him she tipped a pot of tea all over herself this morning, quick, run.'

The doctor arrived, stood by my bed and examined my legs. We told him the teapot story but he did not believe us so we described exactly what happened.

'You will have to go to hospital so I will call for an ambulance.'

When the white ambulance arrived I was taken alone, in my Mr Pastry pyjamas, to St Stephen's Hospital in Wagonbridge. There, as I lay on the stretcher, a nurse took out a pair of scissors and brutally cut my favourite nightclothes in order to remove them as it was impossible to do that any other way. Silently, I swallowed my horror at losing them. The bandages were hard to take off because they had stuck to the blisters. I watched as a nurse placed a long needle to burst the soft, numb, swollen bubbles of skin. It did not hurt at all, though I expected it would. After the initial first aid I was wheeled into the children's ward and laid on a bed without blankets until they admitted me properly then I suddenly saw Daddy enter the ward and my heart sank. I had not been expecting him.

'Who did this?' he demanded.

No other word came from his thin lips.

'Richard, but it was an accident.'

I feared what would happen to my brother when Daddy next saw him. He did not stay long and left without even touching me. Eventually my bed was wheeled, with me aboard, to the left hand side of the ward, half way up. It was not moved again.

Every night at half past seven the matron opened the double wooden doors. I had seen faces looking in through the small round windows. Parents and relatives streamed up the ward to visit their children, hugging them and giving them presents. I sat calmly upright in bed watching them enjoying their time together. Nobody came to my bed with anything. For weeks I was left alone at visiting times but one evening I could take the rejection no longer so fixed my eyes on a particular couple as they came through the doors and insisted with only the power of my gaze, *You are coming to see me tonight.* They followed the invisible, silent magnet right up to my bed and I wondered if they should really be there at all. My shock was hidden but I received them hungrily. Perhaps they were angels sent by God to visit the abandoned child.

'Hello!' They smiled.

I welcomed them sheepishly and took a small wicker basket from the lady's outstretched hand. *I could put a small bag of sugar in there.* Then the man gave me a wind up toy. I held the rough plaited handle of the basket while the man wound up the toy soldier so it could walk. I loved boys' toys too. It was a sad thing to see them leave after such a rare taste of kindness.

The following morning I was overjoyed by another act of love that came through the post. A huge brown parcel addressed to me was brought to my bedside by a nurse. Inside were drawings and messages made by all the children from my class at school. Then a few evenings after my visitors, a nurse wearing a red cloak came and sat by my bed.

'You don't get any visitors do you?' she asked compassionately.

'No.'

'Well, I'll be your visitor. I'll come and see you whenever I can.'

She did not come again. Though I waited and trusted, she broke her promise.

After about two weeks on the ward two nurses took me into the medical room, which was next to my bed, to change my dressings. The taller nurse reached out towards the dressings. I watched her peel back and remove them. A fresh dressing was then applied.

'There you are. Now try to stand up.'

My legs were too weak. I plonked back down and was carried back to bed.

The next morning after waking I was handed a freezing cold metal bedpan. After I sat on it I discovered something hard on the sheet, I had soiled the bed in my sleep! Quickly taking hold of the dreaded object I shoved it into the pan. Fear spread over me like a

monstrous blanket about to suffocate. *I hope they don't find out.*
Later, while the nurse was bed bathing me she found enough
evidence to have me flogged but quickly mentioned it, washed
me and said no more. What I feared of a major punishment for
what I had done, quietly vanished. Only confusion took its place.
Another night, when all was dark, I stretched towards my locker
and, to quench my thirst, felt for the handle of the jug and then
the glass. I poured until sensing the glass was full. The cold water
had reached to the top and I took a much needed drink. When
light dawned and I had woken up, a cleaner shouted,

'Where has all this water come from? It's all down the ward!'

I said nothing in response but was sure they had already traced
the stream to me.

After what seemed a month I was able to have a big bath. The
shallow, warm water felt strange after bed baths every day. The
nurse washing me stooped down after noticing a big, bluish
purple mark on my back and asked,

'Does your dad hit you?'

'Yes,' I answered, not quite understanding.

She thought it was a bruise. I had not connected the two when
she queried so did not explain that it was a birthmark.

A few days later I was surprised to see Daddy walking up the
ward towards me but he had a woman with him. She reached my
bed first and I guessed instantly who it was but still was not
entirely sure.

'Do you know who this is?' Daddy asked.

'No.'

'She is your Aunty Jean.'

Her time with me was short and sweet and I loved her being
there. On her way out I watched as a baby threw its small white
blanket over its cot sides. Aunty Jean threw it back. The baby
loved the game and threw it back out. Aunty Jean laughed as she
hurled it a second time then walked away and disappeared
through the doors with Daddy.

Finally, the day came for me to leave the hospital. I had
witnessed parents collecting their children and the children's
reactions when they turned up to take them home. One girl ran
with so much excitement up to her parents when they came for
her. A parent did not come for me but when I saw Alan, who was

53

now twelve, I grabbed the other girl's actions for myself and ran to meet him but he seemed unmoved by my fast approach. Internally, I stopped, deeply disappointed at his lack of outward affection. I got dressed and feeling strange wearing the clothes he brought in a carrier bag, having been in my nightclothes for so long, we both left the hospital in an ambulance. When we reached home I stepped from the ambulance into a crowd of neighbours I had never met. They had gathered round to see what was happening. It was not a welcome party as none of them showed any sign of warmth, though none were cold either, just curious. Peggy soon told me she also had gone to the hospital after being knocked down by a car. It had not been serious so she went home that very day. My head spun as I took in the news. That should never happen to my sister and I wondered how she could be in the same building without my seeing her.

A few weeks later, on a Saturday afternoon, Samantha went missing. Daddy was worried and called the police but she came home while they were on their way to our house. He took hold of Samantha by the hand and led her to the front room window.

'Do you see that black car? That is the police looking for you,' he said sternly.

'It's ringing its bell,' I joined in.

'You must never go anywhere ever again.' Daddy said.

We could not understand why he was worried when she was home again safe and sound. She had only been next door but one with a lady we called Aunty Gail.

Back at school Peggy and I hung around together at playtimes; we sat on a bench and coloured in our colouring books, never once going over the lines, while our school friends admired our work and made us feel proud. Sometimes we played on the bars, joined in skipping or French skipping and other games. During a game of chase one morning Peggy was bullied by a boy called Edward, who was not English. She came to me with her predicament and I ran after him shouting,

'You leave my sister alone!'

He did and it never happened again.

At the end of the school year, reports of how we performed were sent to Daddy but the year after Mummy died mine did not please him. I had not understood the report except that it was bad. How could I have been bad? He told me off without relaying what the report said and did not tell me what I should do to get a better one next time.

That Sunday Daddy took me to church on the back of his motor scooter. My arms held on tight around his waist in case I fell off. People from church commented in admiration at my experience. Sometimes he allowed all three of us girls to ride on his scooter outside our house. I sat at the very back while Peggy sat in front of me. I had to hold onto the strap which lay across the middle of the seat or onto Peggy's waist. Peggy sat behind Daddy holding onto his waist and Samantha stood on his foot part at the front but we did not go far on those occasions.

Shortly after my hospital stay there was a knock on our front door. A lady had come to see Daddy. Dressed in grey she entered the front room and they closed the door. About a quarter of an hour later Daddy called Peggy and me in and asked,

'Would you like to go and live with Aunty Jean?'

'Yes, yes, yes.' my excited voice answered.

I jumped up and down as high as I could; no more getting into trouble but at the same time I felt silent compassion for Daddy. I felt sorry for how he might feel because we would not be there anymore. The lady stayed silent. Not many days later Peggy and I were on our way to a new life. We left with our few clothes, verbal instructions from Daddy and our Child Care Officer on the train to Aunty Jean, Uncle Sean and our four cousins. 14 Dewhurst Road, Haywick, Hampshire, was our new home. That first night Deborah and Gillian showed us the bathroom. It was strange but pleasant. They had Punch and Judy toothpaste. I had never seen toothpaste before so was not sure how to use the tube. A bar of soap was all we had at home, the same bar that washed us. Craig and Archie accepted us with excitement as much as we did them. Craig was almost my age and Archie only two.

In time we began to enjoy our new life. Uncle Sean played pat a cake hands every day. On Saturdays he mowed the lawn leaving mounds of grass. Our cousins, Peggy and I loaded the wheelbarrow with the clippings before taking it to the bottom of the garden.

We went to new schools. Daddy had specifically instructed me,

'Tell Aunty Jean I said you are to go to a Catholic school.'

I did tell her, still thinking that I was Mummy and in charge. Kneeling beside me she gently rubbed my waist and assured me we would be alright in the schools we would be going to. Deborah, Craig and I went to Toshby Primary School. Craig, who walked with a limp because of polio, carried his violin every day. The highlight of our journey was the bus sucking our bodies into the seats as it hurtled a roundabout. I did not like my new school. Two girls, one with white hair and the other black, made a point of making fun of me. I did not like the one with the black hair. At playtimes I kept myself to myself. Hidden away in my own world I found some little red spiders crawling along the playground wall. By accident I squashed one with my finger. I had not felt anything but saw my finger had a small red spot. As I seeped deeper into myself I started to squash the little mites one by one until the top of my finger was covered red completely. It became my playground pastime. I felt a soothing comfort from the constant repetition. It kept me protected from the rest of the school. When the girl with the black hair left, the other girl and I became the best of friends.

Deborah, aged nine, who I greatly looked forward to seeing, had short, dark hair. At first we got on well but later on at school I suffered some bullying from her. Especially when she found out I had been telling lies about leaving and had said because of that I could not go on the school outing. She and a friend from her class came to me while I was alone in the playground. They told me the teachers would come and prod me with pointed, wooden sticks. They made the gestures that I could expect and I believed every word.

After school Aunty Jean cooked the tea and I was happy again. On Saturdays if there was a choice to be made of puddings Craig and I requested lemon meringue pie every time and at breakfast there was a choice of marmalade so it had to be Golden Shred with the golly on the jar. I liked Craig very much. However, in the mornings I suffered excruciatingly through both him and Peggy as they raced into my room and like gigantic springs bounced all over me in bed. They were laughing but I was having no fun.

'Get away, stop it,' was all I could shout.

Aunty Jean must have been always sleeping as there was no sign of her and consequently I was left to the terrifying awakening every day.

Gradually Peggy and I learned to play simple tunes on the piano. Mummy could play our piano really well at home but we had not been taught, except tunes my brothers had learned off by heart. Aunty Jean's kindness had a good effect. One day she took me to the dentist. We did not wait too long before my name was called. I followed a lady to the dentist's room.

'Sit in that chair, Rachel,' the dentist pointed to the gigantic object. I obeyed but when he said, 'Open your mouth wide so I can see,' I did not obey.

I sat with my mouth firmly closed and when he approached, clad in his white jacket, I saw a monster. He would not be doing me any good. I shook my head from side to side without a word. Trying to calm me with further attempts of gentleness did nothing to prize my jaw open. I won the battle and he let me go. Fearful of Aunty Jean's reaction I squeezed into myself but she said nothing. During our walk home I expected a smack across the head or a severe telling off but it did not come.

Aunty Jean looked after us well. She had even taken Peggy and me shopping to buy new clothes. We looked smart in our new navy blue, pleated tartan skirts and white blouses. As a result of her kindness I wanted a closer relationship with her so one day, while she was in the kitchen and we were in the lounge, I whispered to Peggy,

'Peggy, can you ask Aunty Jean if we can call her Mummy?'

'No, you do it.'

'Oh, please, I'm scared.'

'Well, I am too.'

'Let's ask her together at the same time then.'

'Alright.'

We approached the kitchen sheepishly and with heads slightly raised, mumbled,

'Can we call you Mummy?' our voices synchronised.

'Yes, of course you can.'

Why had we been so afraid?

At weekends we played card games and I lost every one! In the end I was so upset that I did not want to play anymore. They might have let me win one.

Happiness was a rare visitor to my life. It was not an exception when I was invited to a girl's birthday party. Aunty Jean bought a beautiful white dress and put it on me. I loved it but sadness hid my joy. When I arrived at the party both adults and children became involved in games quite naturally. I stayed on my own. Eventually, a man called me over to him,

'Aren't you enjoying yourself?'

'No.'

His compassion touched my heart but no response came from me. I wanted to go home to be with my family. At school I continued to tell the people,

'I'm leaving soon.'

It was not true. Nothing had been arranged for such a thing. My words soon did come true though to my absolute surprise. The following week we were told we would be going to live in a children's home near our family. We had to wait for the school year to finish. The home would be going on holiday to Rinton Bay and we were going with them.

Before we left, Aunty Jean took us by ferry to see our Grandparents on the Isle of Wight. Granddad was very quiet, never saying a word to either of us. He was often busy getting the church ready for services. We attended the morning service at his church on Sunday. I watched him stroll down the outer aisle quite a distance from us. After church and dinner Granny played pick up sticks and other games with us. We only stayed with them for one night. I slept alone in Granddad's study feeling a bit cramped on a camp bed; the room was covered from floor to ceiling with books all the way round and I wondered what was written in them. Did they have any pictures? I was sorry to be leaving the next day. We loved Granny. She was gentle and always had a smile for us.

I do not recall the day we left Aunty Jean but was happy to be leaving the problems with school and Deborah behind.

What was a children's home? What would it be like there? But I was ready to leave and see my family again. We had lived with Aunty Jean for six months.

Chapter Three

In State Care

We arrived without incident at the children's home in Meeking Road, Blackbridge Cross, Kent, later that August. It had been decided that we should not go on holiday with the home after all for reasons unbeknown to us. The top half of the big house was painted white and the remainder plain brick. Neither of us could imagine living there. The average sized front garden path did not take us long to walk down. Our Child Care Officer, Miss Boskin, rang the door bell, to which a member of staff let us in and showed us around the house. Miss Boskin had already explained that we should call the staff 'Aunty' or 'Uncle'. The chief member of staff was known by her formal name, Mrs Frimley. She was a largish lady with short, dark hair and glasses; a kind but strict looking woman who mostly kept in the background.

Lots of children and a couple of members of staff sat waiting at the dining room table for us to join them. Daunted by so many people I shrunk into my shell. The first supper meal in our new home filled me with horror. *What do I do? How am I supposed to hold my cup? What if they don't pick it up by the handle?* I waited thirstily for what seemed an eternity. My eyes slowly roamed the table for the slightest hint as to how they drank from the cups then one of the staff did pick his up by the handle and I quickly followed suit. As I swallowed the milk I wondered what life would be like from then on.

Peggy's and my hair was quite long so within a week we were taken to our first experience at a hairdresser to get it cut short. I sat hearing the snip of the scissors chop my golden hair. The hairdresser could not see the recollections going on inside my head as I stared into the mirror; how I brushed my hair a hundred times at home to make it shine. With my fringe covering my face, hiding it from my sisters, I raised my paws and with a slow, growling roar crept up on them,

'I'm a lion, grrr.'

'All done!' the hairdresser announced.

I snapped out of my dreaming. She held a mirror up so I could see the back. It was a simple but neat style to just below my ears. I was like Goldilocks before that haircut and back at school there was a poster on the wall about the 'little girl who had a little curl right in the middle of her forehead. When she was good she was very, very good but when she was bad she was horrid'. I had had a little curl in the middle of my forehead sometimes too and wondered if I was horrid. I recoiled at the thought, never wanting to be horrid but having a curl there and a poem with the description of that little girl; it must have been me. Next, Peggy had her hair cut. It did not hurt in the slightest when my hair was cut so I did not know why Peggy cried. I thought we were only supposed to cry when something hurt our bodies.

'Why are you crying?' I asked her.

'I don't want my hair cut short.'

'It's ok, it will grow back again.' explained the Aunty who had taken us.

Everybody repeated that it would grow back again and eventually Peggy stopped crying but I wondered why we had to have it cut in the first place if it was only to grow again and how the staff were quite happy to let it.

After adjusting to our new home we had yet another move to an assessment home in Terton, Kent, known as Brierswood. We were going further away from home again. I did not want to go there but to go home. On arrival, taken there by our Child Care Officer in a car, I quickly asked,

'When will the conference be?'

We had been told there would be one where they discussed what would happen to us. I hoped Miss Boskin would take us right back home and not back to Meeking Road children's home. We had never seen such a tall, dark house. It was in the countryside and made of stone and huge windows. I felt a million miles from anywhere. We were left to get used to another new routine.

One morning, after waking up time, Peggy was still fast asleep. Without the covering of blankets she lay on her tummy with her wet pyjamas stuck to her; her bottom stuck in the air *(she had wet the bed since being really tiny)*. One of the Aunties marched right in and gave her an almighty whack. I was horrified as I watched her cause my sister so much pain. Peggy cried for a long time. Especially with wet pyjamas it stung much more than with dry ones. Once she recovered and we were dressed we went together downstairs for breakfast, bubble and squeak plus a fried egg were normally on the menu. I loved the cabbage and potato freshly heated and browned from the frying pan. It was never any good though without tomato ketchup.

A week after we arrived, a member of staff announced,

'A coloured boy is coming this afternoon. You must not stare or make fun of him. He is just a normal boy.'

I waited for him to arrive but by five o'clock, when he still had not come, I asked,

'Where's the coloured boy, isn't he coming?'

'There he is.' Uncle Dave replied, pointing towards the boy.

'He's not coloured, he's brown,' I said, shocked.

I had been expecting a vertically striped boy of many colours, like a stand up rainbow.

At meal times all the children lined up to enter the dining room but were not allowed in until the minute the food was ready. It was my turn to bang on the round, brass gong. I waited at the front of the queue to be told when to hit it and wondered why we had to wait so long for our food as it was usually on time. Nobody notified me so I kept waiting and half an hour later Uncle Dave came out and with a stern voice asked,

'Why haven't you rung the gong? The dinner has gone cold.'

I had not been aware of the correct procedure and did not think a telling off was in order because I had not intentionally missed it.

On weekdays, school lessons were held in either one of two classrooms located up some steep steps and an embankment opposite the main house. At weekends if it was raining there were games in the hall. One game was that the children sat on the floor and so did the teacher facing us. A massive jar of sweets stood on the floor in front of him.

'Close your eyes and no peeping.'

He placed a set of keys on the floor in a random spot then instructed a member of staff to take a child, who would be heading for the sweet, outside the room to be blindfolded. The teacher chose another child who was sitting down to come and get the sweet and then let the blindfolded child in who, after entering the room, had to point to where they thought the child was. If they pointed correctly the other child had to stop and sit down again. The sweet was given to the blindfolded child instead. When Peggy was blindfolded she pointed to the mobile child correctly first time and every time but it was pure guesswork. Each time, Peggy was given a sweet and the poor child trying to get it had none. When it was my time I pointed nowhere near the child who was trying to get to the sweet and never got one. I became quite frustrated with the game. Sometimes Peggy had as many as four sweets in her hand and was willing to share with me.

As we settled into the routine playtimes became fun. We learned to walk on stilts. Pauline, the liveliest child, could do it without any trouble whatsoever but I fell off each time. Putting one foot on one stilt was easy but getting the other foot off the ground was a different matter. Once I did get on them my arm could not keep the second stilt still but waved it about as I tried to balance. As a consequence I fell off every time. As with most things I soon got the hang of it and walked up the steps and down easily on my long wooden legs. Going up was by far the easiest. Coming down, I feared falling head long onto the waiting concrete.

When our six weeks at Brierswood was over we returned to Meeking Road and continued at our old school, St Catherine's. The headmaster called me into his office at the start of the school year and explained that he was putting me up a class. I insisted,

'But I'm in Jackie Walcox's class.'

He would not hear it and explained it was because of my birthday being on September 15th. It had something to do with my age at the beginning of the school year. I was to join junior two. Jackie's sister Julie was in that class. I liked her. Feeling sad at having to leave my other class I had to get to know a whole new lot of children. Jackie had invited us to her house in Hedge Road just before last Christmas. Her youngest sister Miranda was there. She was in Peggy's class and a very pretty girl. We loved her as much as we loved Samantha.

'Mummy, can Rachel and Peggy have a chocolate from the tree?'

'Yes, of course they can.'

Such generosity from parents towards their children was hard to understand. It was not even Christmas Day and we could have a chocolate from the tree.

Samantha had been attending Peach Hill kindergarten before joining us at St Catherine's. Peggy and I were proud of her and always talked about her on the way to school. It was a treat to see her as we did not live with her anymore. At dinner times the first thing I did was scan the dining room to see where she was sitting and waved if she was looking in my direction. Peggy and I always sat together. I was an inquisitive child and wanted to know what would happen if I... Peggy put her dinner down on the table next to me and before she could sit down I pulled her chair away, meaning no harm. She sat and naturally missed her chair. I learned that she first of all got a big shock and second that I got into a lot of trouble. The result was just as much a shock to me as it had been to her. Once I knew the consequences I never did it again.

In the mornings during the winter months my concentration in the lessons came to an abrupt end when the milkman brought in crates of frozen solid milk. At first the bottles were left to thaw out naturally, which I much preferred, but the teacher changed to putting the crate on top of the huge black boiler at the far end of the classroom, giving the milk a horrible luke warm taste. I do not recall him having a bottle to drink. Nobody complained so that was the way it remained.

One boy I sat next to in class became my friend and I soon had him good at arithmetic. Mr Cartwright sat at his desk with the answer book open and only helped the children who queued up on his left hand side. I went up and realised that he did not want to help me as I was on his right. Standing close to him I peered down onto the open book. *I can read the answers.* Tucking them away in my memory I sneaked back to my desk and relayed them to Paul.

'You go next. All you have to do is look at the book and then come back and tell me. We'll get them all right.'

Mr Cartwright did not take the slightest bit of notice. After arithmetic we had Catechism lessons. Our small grey books with red writing on had to be learned off by heart but I could only learn the first three questions. God made me because He loved me and wanted me to be happy with Him in this world and forever in the next.

Back at the home one Saturday a couple came to visit. They sat in the lounge and talked to some of us in order to choose which children to take home with them on future Saturdays. The tall, thin man sat on the settee next to his much smaller but plumper wife. Most of their time was spent talking to Peggy and myself and they decided we would be the ones they took out every week. We were so excited to be the ones chosen.

'What do we call you?' I asked.

'I am Uncle Len and she is Aunty Mo.'

On the first Saturday at their home Uncle Len played golf and prepared his front room for us to have a go. He made a short tunnel in the fireside rug by placing a glass underneath the middle section. We had to hit the ball into the glass with a golf club. All sorts of other activities made our lives better. He also performed all kinds of magic tricks. One of my favourites was the rope that had been cut in two. He showed us the cut ends that were both above and below one of his hands then said the magic word,

'Abracadabra.'

Placing his other hand just above the two cut ends he gradually ran it down to the other end and when he opened it a single rope appeared.

Three months into our stay at the home it was time for our first Christmas. We were invited to a party on a ship at the local dockyard. I was impressed by the naval uniforms the stewards and captains wore. Peggy sat next to me at a long, narrow table set with all sorts of Christmas food and drink and the children sitting opposite us at the same table were very close, so close we could almost touch noses. The only disappointment was that everything about the ship was grey. Not much colour except the food, crackers, party hats and the Naval uniforms with the gold stripes.

All the children from the home loved Uncle Len and Aunty Mo. Peggy and I were not the only ones chosen but none of the others came out with us on a Saturday. Rosy, a quiet, older girl with auburn hair, joined us for the second Christmas at their house and as we lay in bed, pretending to be asleep, the door opened. I narrowly opened my eyes and saw Father Christmas step into the room.

'Are they all asleep?' Father Christmas asked, 'Have they been good all year?'

'Oh yes, very good,' answered Aunty Mo.

Satisfied with that, I tried to sleep. The stone hot water bottle Aunty Mo had filled was immovable and far too hot so was in my way of getting into a comfortable position. Even though my feet were cold I could not put them on the bottle without putting socks on first to prevent them from burning. We dropped off to sleep quite easily after Father Christmas left. A few short hours later it was morning. Peggy and I woke up before the adults. At Peggy's suggestion we dashed down to the front room. On opening the door we came face to face with two unwrapped dolls standing on top of other wrapped presents. Aunty Mo galloped downstairs after us and with a real telling off sent us straight back to bed. When we got up later on no more was said about our earlier rising. Uncle Len handed us our presents. Father Christmas had brought me a knitting set and I learned from Aunty Mo how to knit a pair of mittens for my new doll, Pauline, to keep her hands warm. Peggy got a nurses uniform and looked smart wearing the white cap with the huge, red cross on the front. Uncle Len had made us wooden boxes with matching lids, each with our names painted on the front. We were delighted with those and treasured them. We had a lovely day.

One Saturday, a few months after Christmas, I walked into the bathroom to go to the toilet when, opening the door, I had the shock of my life; Uncle Len was lying in the bath soaking,

'Sorry Uncle Len!'

I shut the door quickly, embarrassed and a little confused as to why he was having a bath in the middle of the afternoon in broad daylight.

'It's alright,' he answered.

But it was not alright for me. Why did he say it was alright when nobody likes being seen in the bath without clothes on, even if they were covered in bubbles?

Another Saturday Uncle Len asked if he could cut off some of my hair.

'I will put it in a plastic paperweight for you to keep forever.'

He worked with plastics. Aunty Mo got some scissors and cut a lock off for him. I was greatly looking forward to seeing my hair encapsulated. For many, many weeks following I pestered him with,

'Where is my hair?'

He constantly assured me it was on its way. My golden sample of hair had been gone for so long and I was getting worried that it would never come back but it did and when I saw it I thought the yellow base was not the right colour to choose for my hair. I said nothing, hiding my disappointment; blue or green would have been better. The transparent domed top showed my lock clearly and I was at least happy to have it in my hands.

One of the girls in the home, Monica, a girl our age and who had mousy coloured hair, was backward. We had to be careful as she scared us. She and Peggy went to the park one afternoon and I followed on later. By the time I arrived they were high up a tree. I strained my neck to see Peggy in Monica's grip.

'She's going to strangle me!' shouted Peggy.

'I'll go and get somebody!'

Running as fast as I could I dashed into a corner shop and told the shopkeeper,

'There's a girl up a tree with my sister and she is going to strangle her.'

The alarmed man came running out. He could not coax Monica down. I felt helpless to save my sister but with some patience and determination the man did get them down and Monica was in a lot of trouble when she got home. At least Peggy was still alive!

Both mornings and afternoons during school holidays some of us played on the pavement outside the home which led to the park at the bottom of the road. It was a long, steep hill so we borrowed a skate from somebody and placed a large book on top of it. Monica, who had since made up with Peggy, demonstrated and another child used the other skate and book to race down the hill with her. We watched as they pushed the pavement away with their hands, lifted their feet and whizzed down the hill. Once at the bottom they walked back to Peggy and I who were waiting for our turn. We mounted the new toy and took off. The intermittent sound of the wheels riding over the gaps in the paving slabs had a calming effect and reminded me of my mother pushing me in the pushchair when I was a toddler and how I especially looked forward to riding over the smoother pink slabs.

Sometimes Peggy and I went to the park on our own. I was convinced Scamp must still be somewhere even though our mother had been gone for two years already. I stood on the swing, holding on tight, and called,

'Scamp, Scamp, where are you?'

I shouted over and over but he did not come and therefore, neither did our mother.

A few nights later I dreamt Jesus set the table for breakfast. He made a good job of the setting and invited Peggy and myself to sit down when we entered the kitchen. Once sitting we waited in expectation for Him to give us something to eat but He did not. He stood leaning against a cupboard where we could see Him but offered us nothing. The table remained set and empty for the entire dream. That was the second disappointment I had of Him and so disappointment became something I expected. After all if Jesus was disappointing me it must have been His will for my life.

During the school holidays whilst out in the garden I discovered a hedgehog and kept him as my pet. Donald, a boy of my age at the home, liked him too or so it seemed. One day after the holidays I came home from school to be told by one of the staff,

'Your hedgehog is dead. Donald stuck some nails in him.'

The loss of my hedgehog made me think twice about finding another one. I felt as though the nails had gone through me.

Time went by and we settled but did not stop longing for home. Never a day went by that I did not have scabs on my cheeks where I constantly dug my own fingernails into them till they bled. Then I had an idea; we would go back home without anybody knowing. We had not seen our family for such a long time. After working out how to get there we arrived at our front door. Alan answered and we were soon having tea with our family once more. It was so good to be home with them again. Daddy was upstairs unawares. But a sudden knock at the front door disturbed our meal. Who could that be? Daddy came down and opened the door to the dark outside.

'I'm one of the staff from Meeking Road. Are Rachel and Peggy here?'

Peggy and I stared from where we sat across the hall in disbelief at the tall, familiar looking lady. She was my favourite member of staff from the home and had been sent to fetch us.

'Can't we stay here?' I asked.

The answer was no and so off we went on the long disappointing walk back to Meeking Road with Aunty Sheila.

For some reason, possibly that of going home without permission, I had to move to a different bedroom from the other children for two weeks and slept in a smaller room with a nineteen year old girl who I was petrified of. One morning I woke earlier than her and my doll *(a different one from Pauline)* made a noise when she turned over. That morning her cow like sound woke the lady up,

'Shut up!' she hissed.

The fear of my father hurriedly surfaced and I lay in a death like brace for what seemed an eternity. I dared not get out of bed and my doll had not meant to move. I could not stir again until the lady got up and left the room. I hated my two weeks in that room and was relieved when I could go back to the others.

A few months later the news came that Daddy and the rest of the family were moving to Cheshire. How exciting!

'Daddy is going to move to C H E S H I R E,' I spelled out when next visiting the Freep's shop. I thought I was still keeping it a secret by not actually saying where my family were going and thinking they could not spell it. And so my father, three brothers and Samantha moved in November but Peggy and I stayed at Meeking Road. Such a distance between us caused a feeling of great abandonment. I was told an address that they had moved to so decided to knit a scarf for William. Not knowing his neck size I used the fireplace hearth to measure the scarf. Twelve fawn tiles length should be enough. When finished I parcelled it up and sent it to the address I had in my mind. He never received it. I also wrote letters to my father but he did not reply.

Peggy and I waited ten long months before moving to a children's home nearer our family, though not as close as in Kent,. We spent a lot of that time helping shovel chalky mounds of earth with some workmen that Peggy had found along Witley Road. They were kind to let us help and said what great little workers we were. The staff at the home never found out. When it was time for us to be leaving for Cheshire we told the men and they were sad both with and for us. I was also sad to be leaving St Augustine's school and the priest (*accompanied by his faithful boxer dog*) who sometimes picked us up, together with other pupils, in his white van from a local shopping centre.

The day Miss Boskin came to collect us tears told of the grief that shattered what had become familiar to us. Uncle Len, Aunty Mo, all the staff and children came to see us off. As we left the front door the comfort of knowing we would be closer to our family helped ease the pain. After our goodbyes we waved from the back seat of the blue mini until everyone was out of sight.

Chapter Four

Lincrest Children's Home

It was a beautiful sunny Wednesday in September, five days before my tenth birthday. Half way through our journey we got out of the car and picnicked at the side of the road. Whilst sitting on the lush green grass with our sandwiches at the ready, I gasped,

'Look at all the ants!' as they appeared from nowhere.

'We better pack up and eat in the car. Come on,' said Miss Boskin.

The ants had not been invited but since they were there first and maybe for many weeks before, they were allowed to have their territory back.

'You have to call the nuns, Sister,' Miss Boskin explained once we were safe inside the car.

Peggy and I pulled funny faces at each other.

'Sister?' we both chanted.

'Yes and the one in charge is called Mother.'

'Mother?'

We laughed. The journey of nine hours was over too soon. It was six o'clock when we arrived at the big, black front door of Lincrest in Campton Range, Sunbarton, Lancashire. The size of the place staggered me. It was much bigger than either Meeking Road or Brierswood. A black iron staircase ran up the outside to the top and a huge tree stood overshadowing the entrance to the back garden.

'Why are there stairs on the outside?' I asked Miss Boskin.

'It's a fire escape.'

Perhaps that was why I saw steps running up the side of the gas containers in Trinton that day but if nobody lived there why were they there? I hoped there would never be a fire.

Before we were even out of the car the front door opened. We were frightened. I bravely faced the newness of the situation but Peggy cried, refused to get out of the car and when she finally did, ran round the pathway leading to the side of the house. After catching her and calming her down Peggy and I set our eyes on our very first nun.

'Hello, I'm Miss Boskin,' said Miss Boskin as the nun reached out to shake her hand.

'This is Rachel, whose birthday is next week and this is Peggy. I'm sure they will settle down well soon enough.'

Peggy and I looked at each other. I put my arm round her shoulders.

'My name is Mother Richard,' the nun grinning at us announced, making her freckles stretch a little.

I never knew nuns had freckles. She seemed a kind person. After some tea and cakes she showed us around the house. There were two group rooms for the children, one either side of the spacious, wooden floored entrance hall. Children were assigned to either the big group room on the right hand side of the hall or the small group room on the left. Peggy and I were put into the small group room to start with and were under the care of Sister Agatha.

We started our new school almost straight away at St John's Roman Catholic Primary. I entered junior three. Peggy went to River House, a separate building for the younger ones. I liked the look of the school. In my block there were two classrooms downstairs and two directly above them. I was in the first room at the top of the stairs. The head mistress, Sister Gregory, was a nun who wore a black and white habit different from those worn by the nuns at Lincrest because they were a different order. A girl called Jane became my first friend so I invited her to my birthday party at the home where she promptly ate most of the sweets.

The first interest outside of the home suggested by Sister Agatha for me was a ballet class in order to improve my posture. She took me there herself. There were a lot of other children between three and eight years old. I felt much taller than they were; after all, I was ten. Wearing my new red ballet shoes I joined in with the first dance.

'Nellie the elephant packed her trunk and said goodbye to the circus,' they sang as we walked round in a circle.

I felt like an idiot being a head higher than the others and not knowing any of the steps. I only went for three or four lessons and then left. On the way back from the last lesson I took a bar of chocolate out of my pocket and ate till I could eat no more then threw the last couple of pieces into the high grass, declaring,

'I'll remember this moment for the rest of my life.'

I still know exactly where that piece of chocolate is. Getting to it now would be impossible unless the flats they have built since are demolished.

The nuns were soon to discover the many talents of Rachel Pallitan. They included the secret of washing socks brilliantly clean but being skillful had its problems. Whilst on holiday the following summer at Healy Bay in Wales Sister Agatha came down with buckets of water for me to wash the dirty socks, stating,

'When you've finished that lot we can go out to the seaside.'

One at a time I inserted a bar of soap into each sock and rubbed them together. This cleaned the inside and the outside at the same time. Getting them so clean gave me a sense of pride and achievement but with every bowl of water thrown down the drain went a few hours of precious childhood. The more I did, the more responsibility I was given. The results were always praiseworthy and honourable but none of that mattered to me.

At Lincrest I cleaned shoes, polished floors with a polisher the size of myself, scrubbed the doorstep while kneeling on hard stone, helped down in the laundry and any other job that needed doing. Something invaded my heart at the same time; a sickly, sweet feeling of 'being good'. I hated the intrusion and tried to destroy it. Whether the feeling was normal or not, I do not know. Had I been trying to snuff out something good and wholesome? As a Catholic I was taught that pride was a sin. It had to go! We were not supposed to feel good. We were meant to go to confession every week and it was difficult if we did not have any 'sins' to confess. I had a standard confession and if the priest was listening to my words week in, week out, surely he knew that this little girl was not coming good. Now and again I invented a new sin to my confession to prevent boredom.

'For your penance say one Our Father, three Hail Mary's and a Glory be,' ordered the priest.

Coming out of the confessional I knelt down in the pew, bowed my head and recited the prayers! It was obvious to me that if I had no sins to confess I would have to stop going to confession and that in itself was a sin. I was trapped in a religious whirlpool.

As well as my 'pride' problem I had a suspicious, detective like mind and beckoned some of the children now and again to the window of our bedroom to call to the murderer hiding outside to come out, that we could see his shirt or his head but he took no notice whatsoever. I thought we could find somebody there and help the police catch the man they wanted on the news.

When Christmas arrived I wondered if Father Christmas knew where we had moved to. Sister Agatha summoned our group,

'Take a pillowcase off one of your pillows and put it at the bottom of your bed, then go to bed and I'll wake you in time for Midnight Mass.'

After Midnight Mass at St John's church and a mince pie we went back to bed. When we woke and explored presents that had been put into our pillowcases most of them were secondhand and not even wrapped. It took the wonder out of my day but I had to be grateful as a good Catholic as any disappointment would be a sign of ingratitude.

Around New Year a lot of the Charity's children's homes were called to go to Pomiston and from the Charity headquarters we sang over the radio to the whole world. Singing our best so that others could hear us there and then was a great joy. Children were meant to be seen and not heard but that day we were heard and not seen!

A few months after Peggy and I arrived a new nun called Sister Robert was introduced to us. She took over the small group room and those of us under Sister Agatha's care moved to the bigger room with her. Sister Agatha described her ultra thin body and white face,

'She has no blood.'

Is she a Martian? A few days after her arrival Sister Robert started to steal clothes from our group to give to the children in hers. I heard from one of them that she also jumped on her children. Even so, we could hear her shouting and punishing them from behind the closed door. I sure was glad not to be in her group. With my sense of injustice I decided she needed to be punished too and the only way I knew was to give her cheek. One day she came into my dormitory and a threat for my audacity was hot on her lips,

'How dare you talk to me the way you do. We'll phone Pomiston and tell them to send you to Cardinal Creek.'

Nobody knew why 'Cardinal Creek' and none of us knew what Cardinal Creek was. But it sent a dull thud to my stomach even if I did not know what to expect if I ever went there. It sounded like a very bad place. At the tail end of her verbal flogging, she added,

'You've got a face like the back of a bus!'

For an adult to speak to a vulnerable, unloved child like that - and coming from a nun - well, she should have known better. The harvest of her words was quickly reaped with,

'Well, you've got a face like the back of a cow in action!'

A Cheshire expression, Kent people would never say such things! That was the end of the battle. She never confronted me again. When she left the room I looked into the mirror above the sinks in our bedroom and thought, *I wonder what I'll look like when I'm twenty, thirty, forty, fifty, sixty, seventy, eighty, ninety, a hundred.*

As well as nun problems Peggy teased me unmercifully most days. The first time one of the Cheshire girls heard me scream, 'Shut up!' she quickly corrected me,

'She's not saying anything.'

'What?'

'You don't say shut up if she isn't saying anything.'

'Well, we always do in Kent.'

But I realized the sense of not saying shut up and stopped. In Cheshire language it meant, 'Keep quiet!' not 'Stop it!' The pronunciation of certain words like butter and grass was also different.

'Butt – er is booter *(short oo)*. Grarse is grass *(as in cat)*', Wendy continued to explain and I remembered Miss Boskin telling us that in the car on the way up.

We picked up the accent over time.

One girl named Deirdre was half cast and a first class bully. We cowered at her presence. She encouraged some children to gang up on others. If she held a grudge against someone, everybody had to. Our bedroom had horizontal iron bars on the windows. Wendy, a girl about my age, accused me one morning,

'You dropped my soap into the gutter.'

'No, I didn't. It must have been somebody else.'

'No, it was you, Deirdre saw you do it.'

'No, she didn't.' I replied angrily.

There was only one thing for it. Walking towards the window I discovered the soap and climbed out between the bars in my pyjamas and while holding onto the bars tightly, dangled my feet down the ridge towards the place it rested. The ridge was a small roof covering our group room's bay window, with a gutter at the lower edge.

'Rachel, come back in. We know it wasn't you,' they panicked.

'No, you said it was me and now I'm going to get it.'

I was not about to give in. They had done the damage. I imagined the nuns rushing out of the front door and looking up at the sight of a brave girl rescuing somebody's soap with her toes which grasped the thin, white sliver and lifted it. Letting go of the bar with my left hand I determined to take hold of the soap with my fingers. My heart beat fast in case I fell to the earth below and hit my head on the protruding rocks. I hated injustice. The girls had to feel the impact of what they blamed me for. Their horrified faces sweat with anxiety. My toes handed the soap to my waiting fingers. As I was pulled back into the room and safety I was told of the plot it had been,

'Deirdre made it all up. She dropped the soap there and made us blame you for it,' Wendy explained.

So I had impressed them with my bold, brave response. The lot of us sent Deidre to Coventry after that, for a week. Coventry is when you do not speak to a person, for whatever reason, for as long as they deserve.

Despite the lack of forgiveness most of us went to every Mass held in the chapel which was located at the left hand corner of the hall, diagonally opposite to the front door. Going to Mass kept God's anger at bay. Together with confession and communion on Sundays and Holy Days of Obligation it would shorten our time in Purgatory when we died. At the beginning of Mass we dashed to the cupboard in the hall, reached to the top shelf for our foam kneelers and raced to be first into the chapel. The partition of the chapel was open for us to kneel at the side of the nuns. We faced them, they faced the altar. At communion the race to be first was just as evident and the eagerness for the Mass to finish could not be hidden as we grabbed our kneelers to return them to the cupboard.

Deirdre, who was older than any of us, decided to watch Alfred Hitchcock on television and roped us all into doing the same. Plans were made for a successful night's viewing. The nuns would never find out. We placed pillows inside our beds and covered them up to fool the nuns that we were asleep. All of us crept downstairs to the big group room.

'I think we should hide behind the legs of the table and chairs till they have gone to bed. When they are asleep we can turn on the telly,' I suggested.

'Well, we don't want to miss any of it. It starts at half past eleven,' said Deirdre.

No lurking adult would detect us behind the furniture. The nuns wandered upstairs to say goodnight and the television would soon be ours to watch in peace. The identical sleeping pillows, however, were immediately discovered! The trooping nuns could be heard getting ever closer. We were sworn to silence, no matter what. I felt sorry for Sister Ann, my favourite nun, in her anxiety but swallowed my compassion and stayed put. They came into the group room in concerned conversation, not realizing that many eyes were watching their feet. They decided to give up their search and phone Pomiston but six year old Diana called out while walking into the hall,

'Sister Ann?'

A trail of other children followed. The nuns roared with laughter as the tension broke and Sister Ann sat on the stairs in relief. We did not get to see even the start of Alfred Hitchcock.

Sister Ann was a pretty nun with a round face and rosy cheeks. She did the cooking and was always in the kitchen when we got home from school. I ran in to her every day at that time with my homework and got to work on it on the kitchen table so I could ask her questions about it. She was the gentlest of all the nuns and always thought before she spoke so never uttered a word that would hurt anybody. That is why I loved her. She was a great example to me of how I wanted to grow up.

I rarely, if ever, smiled. One regular visitor to the home, Mr Crefford, jutted out his bottom lip whenever he caught sight of me. I smiled then. He was taking the micky but it achieved what he wanted, albeit short lived. If he traced the pouting lip to its source, he would have found a broken heart.

The dejected brood at Lincrest soon hatched another plan. We decided to run away a few weeks after being moved into the bedroom across the landing, where the fire escape doors in the corner of the room were. The ones who did not want to come were sworn to secrecy. In the thick of night we got dressed, leaving our pyjamas on under our clothes, but Peggy dressed in full school uniform, tie and all. As quiet as mice we tiptoed towards the fire escape door. Wendy pushed the bar while listening for the slightest sound in the silence. Clank, it responded, and opened. We all piled onto the black, iron platform. Peggy was on the second step down and in her anxiety turned to me, exclaiming,

'Maybe somebody's heard us?'

'No, Sister Agatha can't have. She's right up the top,' I quickly looked up to where her room was, 'and there's no light on.'

It was only one floor up but her tiny window made it look further than it was. The boys slept on that floor also.

'Quick, get back into bed!' whispered Wendy's unexpected voice from behind; she was the last one out, 'I can hear her coming.'

She pulled the door shut quickly after the six scampered back in. In a second our heads were under the covers and eyes closed as we listened, breathing heavily. Peggy's bed, next to the door, was nearest Sister Agatha and as she was second to last in did not have enough time to change back into her pyjamas, she should have left them on underneath like everyone else. The rest of us took our clothes off from under the blankets and left them inside the bed. Sister Agatha opened the door to the 'sleeping children' and before we could sigh with relief, she snapped,

'What was that noise?'

Nobody stirred. With one hand she grabbed Peggy's blankets and gave them a quick yank.

'Why are you in bed with all your clothes and shoes on?'

'Sister, I forgot to get undressed.'

Peering out from under our covers we saw Peggy lying in her full uniform. After a brief telling off and a warning that we should not try again to run we were left to sleep soundly for the rest of the night. Nothing at all was mentioned the following day and we were not punished. When we *were* punished by Sister Agatha she would pull our cheeks and dig us with her elbows whilst complaining about her rheumatism. The rope that hung from her waist, the rosary beads and keys that jangled when she moved made me feel tired. Whenever she wanted us, it was mainly for trouble so we decided the best thing was to pull our own cheeks on our way down. It would save her the job. Of course we were a true blessing to her as well and as I was good at cleaning I volunteered to spruce up the white parts of her habit when they changed to a dull, cream colour. The plastic bib and outer part of her veil were made of the same material. I rubbed them clean on a cupboard top outside her room with a cloth dipped in dampened cleaning powder, then rinsed and polished them dry. Nobody could do a better job and no doubt she was glad to have me around.

As time went on we started to feel the confinement of being trapped and unwanted and my behaviour, at least, took a turn for the worse. We older children were given the task of looking after the younger ones if we wanted to. I chose a cute two year old girl who had just arrived. I loved her but in my own confusion I did not know how and so as my father and the nuns had treated me I treated her. Dinner times were punishment times,

'Eat your dinner,' I commanded and tried to feed her but she refused the food. 'Right, let's go to the toilet.'

Once there, I pinched her and told her to eat her dinner or she will get more. I felt the cruelty I had learned from my father rise into my face but when the punishment was over I hugged her; something my father never did.

'You must do as you are told in future and eat your dinner.'

After a week in my charge somebody found a couple of bruises on her. I had been caught and was no longer allowed to look after her. I denied anything to do with the bruises, fearing punishment myself but the look I received from the lady who reported me took on character from her lips,

'I do not believe you in the slightest.'

With the feelings of vulnerability and shame the distance grew between myself and the adults of the home.

Peggy's and my school life: I was a fairly good pupil. My handwriting, being neat, was always praised. Sister Gregory described my work,

'Your English is good but your arithmetic is appalling.'

When I got home, after her exquisite report, I danced in to Sister Ann and repeated the praise I had received,

'Do you know what appalling means?' she asked.

'No,'

I did not get an explanation, just silence in response.

Peggy looked up to me and I looked after her the best I knew how. At playtime one day some of her trust was shattered. In the playground I held my clasped hands in front of me inviting her to run and jump. The children lined up opposite me and behind her to take it in turns. Her clasped hands were ready to rest on mine so I could swing her as I twisted but the inquisitive part of my nature replaced any common sense and I took my hands away swiftly just before she would have landed on my arms, not realizing that she would land flat on her face on the tarmac. I had not expected her to fall but to keep running and anticipated a funny outcome.

Nobody taught us how to behave. Those in authority punished us but never explained why our behaviour was wrong. Without parents I was left to grow wild. Wild does not mean like a cowboy but like a flower on a mountainside without a gardener to care for it, left to the elements to fend for itself; so the behaviour did not improve and the punishment increased!

One morning at school I was caught looking through the glass panel into a classroom by Sister Alice who was the only other nun besides Sister Gregory; they were both of the same order and lived in the same convent round the corner from the school. The class was full of children and in progress. I did not see Sister Alice or hear her hefty frame mounting the stairs behind me. Without explanation she gave me a good hiding whilst standing on my foot. Her full weight on my size two feet nearly crushed them to a pulp. She taught physical education and while learning rounders one afternoon in the playground I, holding the round bat, missed hitting the ball every time. There was just not enough bat to hit the ball with in the first place. For the entire lesson she made me stand on the batting square,

'You will stay there until you hit it.'

I never did and the bell rang before any victory materialized.

On Saturdays the nuns from Lincrest took us to Irish dancing lessons in the centre of Sunbarton. However, they were not the teachers! Diana, who had given up on Alfred Hitchcock, was particularly good. We admired her enormously but could never match her expertise. After we had learned quite a few jigs, single reels and four hand reels we attended Feshes and displayed before judges. In my performances I did not manage to win any medals or be ranked in any position, though on one occasion they told us they were torn as to who the winners would be.

On Whit Sunday we dressed up in our Irish dancing costumes to go on the Whit walks through Cheshire. Deirdre, who was walking right behind me, whispered in my ear,

'You've got a bee on your back,' to make me step out of line.

'You've got a bee on *your* back,' I retorted from in front.

What a day that was. Thousands of children and a huge procession of Irish dance costumes filled the centre of the city with vibrant colour and loud music as the bands played.

During the school summer holidays we went off to Abrisham, Wales; a seaside resort and, after settling down, went on an outing for a day. Walking back through the streets in the evening with my imagination was not a safe thing to do. As I had watched on the news concerning the Ku Klux Klan I was convinced they were coming round the corner with their hoods covering their faces and because we were Catholics, after us! Their crosses aflame we were sure to be burned at the stake. They never showed up but I was always terrified they would and was glad when the holiday was over.

Back at the home the older girls, being more experienced than the younger ones, took a liberty with our naivety. I got into a lot of trouble for mine; after all I was only ten years old. While at a bigger park, further afield from the local one, the older girls beckoned me over to them. I had never been to that park before.

'Rachel, go to those boys and tell them we want to go out with them.'

Gullibly, I trotted off to the gang sitting on the grass.

'You know those girls over there? They want to go out with you,' I seriously and proudly announced, thinking they would be pleased.

One of the boys stood to his feet, advanced towards me and before I knew what was happening picked me up by my ankles, swung me around and let go. The girls showed no sign of having anything to do with it. Nobody came to my rescue and I felt that the whole world was my enemy. Thankfully, I was not physically hurt. I vowed to myself I would never go to that park again.

Peggy's and my new Child Care Officer was a nun. Mother Bede who replaced Miss Boskin was the same order as the nuns at Lincrest. She visited us from time to time and took us to her Convent in Wigan. Peggy had gone somewhere else that day and the place was the quietest I had ever known it. I was expecting Mother Bede to arrive at Lincrest to take me and sat at the bottom of the stairs waiting, as she was late. An hour later I was still sitting in my hat and coat repeating over and over,

"Ring the bell, ring the bell."

My spirits were very low. Nobody came with any news of her whereabouts. Even when Sister Ann saw me sitting there asking where she was she seemed unconcerned and walked straight past me. Mother Bede did not turn up and no explanation was given as to why.

On our birthdays the taxi drivers of Sunbarton came to the home bringing presents. They were brand new and especially chosen for us. I appreciated a Cindy doll they bought me on my eleventh birthday and remembered Daddy taking away my presents at Christmas or my birthday if he thought they were not fit for me. He put them on top of his wardrobe. I wondered if I would ever get them. I was seven the last time he took them. There was never a mention of them since.

As well as our birthdays the taxi drivers used one day of their summer to take us to Flippy Beach or Huckleberry Sands; two hundred black taxies decorated with balloons and streamers in delightful procession. Underprivileged and disabled children from all over Cheshire were treated like VIPs. Taxies honking their horns during the entire journey could be heard for miles. Children, peering through the taxi windows and waving to other drivers as they gave way, beamed excitement all around. It was a special day with rides on roller coasters and all sorts of other attractions.

Buses were not as exciting though and while travelling on the bus on our way back from an outing with the nuns one cloudy afternoon, Peggy wanted the toilet and could not wait. It turned into a kind of, 'can Peggy hold on' game with Sister Agatha, and she was enjoying great success. Never had it been known for her to hold on as much as that. Being pleased with herself she sped up the stairs and hurriedly opened the toilet door. Relief at last! She sat down realizing only too late that she had not lifted the lid but that in no way takes the virtue out her achievement.

It was not often that members of our family visited but when they did it made all the difference. Daddy visited us at Lincrest about three times in those two years. When he came I ran to meet him but standing like a brick wall he stopped me in my tracks. He brought Samantha with him much to my delight and I greeted her as I put my arm round her shoulder. Peggy followed behind but Deirdre was quick to retort,

'You're always getting up first to see your family and Peggy never gets a chance.'

I had never given it a thought. It was not intentional and I certainly did not stop her from coming but I did not do it again. I had wondered why she hardly ever met them with me thinking she simply did not want to. I would have preferred it if she had as I loved my family being together. It was my only real longing, to be one big happy family. My childlike spontaneity became corrupted that day.

Months went by until I was nearly eleven and a half and, as always, only wanted to go home and be with my family. It was nearly time to leave the primary school and go to a new school for older children and I was scared. It was also time to move to a different home for older children. The thought stressed me greatly. A conflict arose. I wanted to go home to be with Samantha or we may never know each other. My youngest sister, what would become of our relationship? I learned what the nuns really thought of me when Peggy told me what Sister Agatha had said,

'If Rachel goes away, tell her she can never come back.'

And so my mind was made up, I would go home, leaving Peggy at Lincrest. How does one decide when there is such confusion in a young life? I would have had to leave anyway so deciding to leave her was not in my hands. She still would have been left there on her own without me... so I left Lincrest and St John's school behind. I would miss the four on a bike rides; Wendy standing up behind the handle bars, pedaling, Peggy sitting on the handle bars, Sylvia on the seat and me on the rear mudguard riding along Lomper Road towards the school and at the sight of a policeman jumping off in all directions leaving innocent looking Wendy to pedal alone. Sylvia was Diana's sister but we were not close friends. I would also miss Sister Ann a lot but not much else. As I waved goodbye I had no idea what kind of life awaited me. I had visited home only once during the summer holidays the previous year and became sick with yellow jaundice. Because of that I had to go back to Lincrest sooner than expected. The doctor came to see me from time to time and I was in bed for six weeks with the illness.

I was told Daddy still got angry but that, I thought, was better than me becoming a corrupted teenager and learning how to smoke, swear and other things I did not care to get involved in.

Chapter Five

Home of Terror and Secondary School

The afternoon of my arrival at home I witnessed a fight between Alan and Richard. Richard whacked Alan so hard across the arm with a snooker cue that the cue broke in half! I wondered what I had walked into and if I was to expect this all the time. My brothers were strangers to me as I had not lived with them since I was eight, except when I came home from Lincrest for that short stay. Alan was in agony for days and the disturbance at home brought my new future into sharp focus.

I was still eleven years old and Daddy decided I should go to St. Peter's R.C. Secondary Modern School in Merwich, Cheshire. As I had no school uniform Daddy gave me a horrible yellow, flower patterned dress to wear; that made me the only pupil in the school without one. It was not for another three years that the school supplied a navy skirt, white blouse and maroon jumper but with no school colours decorating the v shaped neck. Receiving the makeshift school uniform helped my dignity a little but I was still the odd one out with not having the colours on the jumper.

My second introduction to life at home was learning the routine from eight year old Samantha. At six in the morning the alarm woke us. Quickly, we washed and dressed. Once downstairs I was ready for my instructions,

'First, you put the kettle on.' Picking it up Samantha filled it and switched it on. 'Now we have to go round the shop for the paper while the kettle's boiling.' Off we went on a five minute run to buy the early morning newspaper. On our return Samantha put a teaspoonful of tea from the caddy into the warmed pot. Replacing the lids of the caddy and teapot she explained, 'You mustn't let the water go off the boil. Pour it onto the tealeaves while it is still bubbling. Then stir it and leave it to brew for three minutes.'

'Okay.'

I watched hoping to remember it all.

'You pour a cup of tea for Daddy with two sugars and make sure you stir it.' I watched as she left the kitchen with the cup and saucer in her hand. Looking behind she asked, 'Can you get the bread out of the larder?' I reached up to take the Mother's Pride, orange, greaseproof package out of the cupboard. On her return she instructed, 'Take four slices out and spread them thinly with margarine to the very edges of the crust and you can put marmite or meat paste in them. I'll show you.'

While she was demonstrating the exact way to do the job of feeding our father, I asked,

'What do you say to him when you take the cup of tea up?'

'You say, "Good morning Daddy it's quarter to seven, here's a hot cup of tea and the paper." Then you put it down on the bedside table.' *I hope I remember the words.* She carried on, 'When you've done the sandwiches you wrap them in one of these.' She took an old used bread packet out of the draw underneath the larder and laid it out on the dresser. Taking the sandwiches she gently placed them on the greaseproof side of the paper with her tiny hands; once wrapped there was a neat bundle ready for Daddy to pick up, 'You put them on the table next to his breakfast.' I followed her into the front room, not wanting to get anything wrong or out of place. 'If you don't hear any sounds that he is getting up you go back upstairs at five to seven. Tell Daddy it is five to seven and his tea is getting cold. Take with you a hot kettle for his wash and shave.' On this, my first occasion, I went upstairs and performed the ritual of waking him then placed the kettle on the floor just inside the bathroom door. Once downstairs Samantha carried on, 'Then you clean his shoes,' she opened the lid of the high stool where the shoe polish, brushes and duster were kept, 'and make sure they are very shiny. Don't forget to do the soles. There mustn't be any dirt anywhere.' After cleaning them she carried them from the kitchen into the front room and placed them neatly in front of his chair. 'You have to do that while the egg is boiling and it has to be soft in the middle. Then butter two pieces of bread and do them exactly like I've shown you.'

'Does Daddy still go mad every Sunday?' I wanted to know just in case he had changed since I last asked.

'Yes and on other days as well.'

A few minutes later Daddy came down to eat his breakfast of two Weetabix with warm milk, the soft boiled egg, one slice of bread and butter to go with the egg and one with marmalade. We were not free of our morning duty towards him until he left for work at quarter to eight in case he needed anything else. Once he was out of the back door we got on with having our own breakfast of porridge, cooked over the hob for twenty minutes and dished up in bowls for however many there were of us; two wooden spoonfuls each, sprinkled with one teaspoon of sugar. After breakfast Samantha walked to the local junior school five minutes away while William and I took the bus to Merwich. On my first day I was confronted with teasing problems. A couple of the boys approached me and politely asked,

'Will you go out with Shaun?'

'I can't,' I responded gullibly, 'my dad won't let me.'

All they needed to go ahead and take the micky was right there. Not to mention my red hair, glasses and fancy dress.

I sat in class dejected and without friends for many weeks until, one day, I overheard my form teacher asking one of the girls,

'Will you be Rachel's friend?'

So Edith became my friend. Her white hair made her as unique as I was. Her maturity and good nature were admirable. She mixed with others well but I remained a loner. Her many friends sometimes made me feel left out as she was my only one.

Soon the boys gave me a new name, 'Loch Ness,' The Scottish red headed beast had arrived at St Peter's! Perhaps I should have stayed 'loched' away? Or perhaps it was because I was? I never retaliated.

'You don't have to blush?' said William, when he saw them teasing me one time.

'What's a blush?' I asked.

I knew my face got very hot and as often as I breathed sometimes. He did not answer.

Because of our home and school situation Samantha and I wagged school for weeks on end but left the house often in case anybody came home. We had another home in the grounds of the local Children's Hospital which we nicknamed Toy Town. It was well hidden from the main hospital and surrounded by trees and undergrowth. To get there we wandered down a cinder path with its open green spaces. About three quarters along we diverted to the right and, with great difficulty, climbed up a steep embankment to get to the hut. We were constantly aware that we might be caught but risked it anyway. Our dinner money was spent on biscuits, rusks, sweets and fizzy drinks for lunch. It was great fun jumping up and down on an old dismantled piano making all kinds of twangy tunes fill the air. We stayed there until it was time to go home from 'school'. We would return to school for a few weeks before going back to the hut just in case they noticed we were missing. On sunny days while walking home along the cinder path, whether from school or the hut, sunbeams often poured through gaps in the trees. The translucent yellow slides reached the ground without a curve and frightened me. *If I touch them what will they do to me? Will they hurt me or change shape? Will they grab me and make me disappear?* I never stayed long enough to find out.

A year after I came home from Lincrest it was Peggy's time to leave and she came home to live with us. The nuns bought her a uniform so she did not suffer the material poverty or soul suffering as much as I did concerning that. Besides my glasses and other things already mentioned my hands were slightly deformed and people commented on them from time to time. Sometimes, especially when tired, the squint in my left eye turned inwards. I was unaware of it because that eye was also three quarters blind; much less light went into it. Even if there was enough light there was nothing I could do about the hated abnormality. Peggy's arrival gave us more help with the housework and at least our family were all together - ish. William only messed about admiring his muscles and feet. I organized the three jobs so that one job per girl would see the work done by the time our father came in at quarter past five. Sometimes he would come earlier and that left us unprepared. We took the chores in rotation on different days during the week; making up the fire, washing up and cooking, hoovering and dusting.

After school Peggy and I ran the distance of two lamp posts and walked one along the length of Ambury Road up to the cinder path, through the long cinder path *(no lamp posts there)* where halfway along it, every day, for some inexplicable reason, I slammed my satchel onto the ground in utter frustration. It took a while before I was able to pick it up and carry on. Time stood still as it witnessed my outburst. Would I ever go beyond that moment? Deep down inside of me wretchedness also stood still. Peggy stopped and watched helplessly as I refused to move forward to pick it up. I never knew what she thought. It was not about her but maybe something subconscious was going on about home or simply that my life was not worth living. When I finally made it through and time resumed, we carried on to the end of the cinder path then past two sets of houses until finally making it to our maisonettes; a row of houses with another row directly above. We lived in the third house along the bottom row of about eight. Most days we made it home in twenty minutes by twenty past four but sometimes later. I took the key from my pocket and unlocked the back door. We set to work. There were extra jobs at times such as filling the coal bunker which was in the kitchen. It was filled from an outside door on the front doorstep; rather like a stable door, the bottom door of the two was for the dustbin. The only heating was from the open fire in the front room. The fire also heated the hot water via a damper. We used the poker to pull the ring down which opened a vent at the back of the chimney and drew the flames towards the water tank which was definitely not up the chimney but was upstairs, so the whole thing baffled me. I was unable to work the system out. We also made our toast by the fire using a dinner fork as we did not possess a long handled toasting fork. That was pretty hot work but the smoked toast which crackled as it dried over the flames was certainly tasty. Coal was delivered every Tuesday and each grey sack weighed one hundredweight. We untied the sacks, heaved them onto our shoulders and into the top outdoors cupboard from the step. We then lay them down and poured the contents into the coal bunker, all eight of them, one after the other. At first we made a good job of the routine and had everything finished in time for our father's return but Peggy discovered a way of getting an additional education.

'Stop reading the paper, Peggy. You can't read it, Daddy will be in soon.'

'It's interesting.'

'Yes but you can't, you have to empty the ash outside, make the rings, get the coal and light it. You'll never get it done in time.'

She usually did get it done on time but only just. I, however, was constantly glancing out of the front room window at the same time as supervising my sisters. Our father wanted everything done and finished by the time he got home. Whoever's job it was to clean and tidy the kitchen and washing up also had to cook his dinner and have it on the table for when he came in. They did not have the time to do Peggy's job too.

'I have to do my work and Samantha is doing hers. Please finish the fire. What if it doesn't light? You have to have the time to get it lit,' I urged.

My patience and nerves were getting fraught with fear. I was in charge and cannot stress the tension in the house too much for when Daddy got home. If we were to avoid trouble we had to be perfectly behaved, just like in the regimental Royal Navy that he had been accustomed to. With that type of responsibility I needed eyes all around my head, especially from five past five onwards. Never restful anxiety squeezed me into a mold of compliance to him. Clearing the things from Daddy's breakfast was the first thing. If I was working in the kitchen I could not keep an eye on Peggy as easily as in the front room. Samantha always did her work and when Peggy was not doing the fire she also completed her tasks on time. But it was the newspapers that acted like a magnet for her eyes, perhaps not only her eyes but her knees and hands also for she could not get up off the floor until every word was read. When tension accumulated and we had more experience of Daddy's rages I got to the point where I shouted at five o'clock,

'He's here!'

She had to take stock and get on with it. Eventually, I had to resort to hitting her to try to get her to cooperate. But one afternoon she chose not to heed the warning. She was reading as usual. I was exasperated, terror oozed out of every pore of my head but the stubbornness persisted.

'Peggy, get it done now!'

I was constantly looking out of the window for sight of his car. She had not even made one ring out of the sixteen needed! Nor had she emptied the ash, nothing. It did not seem to bother her that we needed the skin on our bodies. She just switched into another world. She laid the doubled sheets of newspaper on the rug ready to fill with ash but that was all. I shouted with my heart in my mouth,

'He's h.e.r.e... q.u.i.c.k...!' After over half an hour of trying to get her to cooperate, I added, '...and I'm not joking.' Then in a more resigned monotone, 'He is turning the car round.'

I was numb with trying. We were in huge trouble. Twelve year old Peggy instantly demagnetized. Samantha and I rolled two sheets of newspaper together eight times each and tied them into rings as fast as we could. Peggy shoveled the ashes from the fireplace into the spread out newspaper on the floor, grabbed the paper both sides so that the ashes would not fall out and rushed down the concrete garden path with the risk of bumping into her father. Samantha and I watched with baited breath. Peggy whizzed back in after emptying the ash into a pothole near his parking space at the bottom of the garden. He was still maneuvering the car and seemed to be taking a lot more time than usual. Peggy ran in, shoved the rings onto the fire grate on top of the paper which hung over the grate; that part was used for lighting the fire from the front. She snatched the shovel, fled into the kitchen, opened the coal cupboard door, rammed the shovel into the pile of coal, rushed back into the front room and shed the coal onto the rings then dashed for another shovelful. Her nervous hands fumbled for a match and lit the fire. At that moment Daddy walked in. In front of his eyes and yet without him noticing, she succeeded. Such was the speed of her movements we still cannot understand how he and Peggy did not collide or how she managed to do a twenty minute job in two. I had never known panic to produce so much order out of chaos.

Some days we invited friends in who lived in the same block of maisonettes. Two and three year olds came in for some fun. Peggy and I picked them up by one arm and one leg, lifted them from the seat of the settee to the top of the settee back and dropped them. Their little faces lit up with laughter as they bounced on the seats. My father, of course, was unaware of what went on behind his back. Some older children came around for a bit of drama during the school holidays and so we amused ourselves. One particular afternoon while we were enjoying the house to ourselves with our neighbours I happened to be looking out of the front room window when I spotted a familiar car pass by at the bottom of the garden,

'Daddy just drove past!' I said in a desperate whisper. I felt the blood drain from my face. 'Quick! You have to go. Whatever you do don't stand up. He can see straight through to the front door. Crawl on your hands and knees.'

Deeply humbled, our friends raced on all fours up the hall and to the front door. The front room overlooked the back garden and the kitchen overlooked the front garden. The kitchen door was at right angles to the lounge door. I leisurely walked into the hall in case he was watching. He would only see one of us. I closed the front room door behind me blocking his view and let our neighbours out. That day served to put us off having other children round too often.

After work and dinner his usual habit was to go up to bed for a lie down. During those times if we as much as talked above a whisper it disturbed him. He knocked on the floor,

'Shh, Daddy's just knocked,' I said. Tense faces and bodies stood to attention.

'No, he didn't,' said Samantha.

'Yes, he did, listen.'

He did not knock again at that time which meant we had been making a little too much noise. We slid into silence and that, he was sure, was good enough not to have to knock again. It was not his usual time to summons us. Sometimes he did knock again and we obediently kept quiet but if he knocked even when we were quiet we knew one of us had to go upstairs to see what he wanted. After his nap a loud bang on the floor froze us to the spot hoping he would not knock again. Our hopes were dashed as the sound of terror struck once more.

'He's getting up now,' I said. 'Will you go up this time Samantha?'

'No, you go up.'

'Will you Peggy?'

'No, I'm not going.'

'Please, Samantha, you go up to him.'

'No, I can't.'

'Please, I'm always going up. Look, I'll make the tea and you take it up. I'll go tomorrow,' I promised.

'Alright,' she unwillingly succumbed. I did not see her again for quite a while. When she came down she put the kettle on a second time without saying a word. I heard it boil from the front room. She made her way back up the stairs and left it outside the bathroom for his shave. At quarter to eight he at last came down to the front room. A smart man in his camel coloured coat or Hartpin's grey suit walked behind the settee where we sat watching television. He stood at the door of the 'shed' *(a room next to the front room where he kept his workbench)* beside the television and gave his orders for the evening,

'Alan, you are in charge. Richard, go to bed at ten. Make sure you go to bed at half past eight Samantha and Peggy at nine. Rachel, you go at half past nine and warm up my bed.'

I smiled to humour him,

'Yes.'

His Brillcreamed hair was combed neatly away from his unsmiling face revealing his high forehead. With his orders given, he turned around and opened the door. I gazed at his unused workbench until he closed the door behind him. When the outer door clicked shut he was gone for the evening. The tension broke into fragile peace as he left the house. His orders had to be kept. Every night was the same. Nothing new ever happened to us unless it was a night of trouble with him. I was happy on the nights he did not ask me to warm up his bed. I tried to avoid his gaze on his way out so he would forget to ask. When that happened I went to my bed and slept. About midnight, when he came home, he walked silently into our bedroom. Peggy and Samantha slept and so did I until his arms reached into my bed and gripped my small body. Pretending to be asleep I floated freely across the room on his forearms. He carried me out of the room and into his bed. As I lay there my tense emotions screamed silently for help. I listened as he got undressed and ready for bed and, once there, he ran his finger over the contour of my face. By then he knew I was awake and dictated,

'Say I love you, Daddy.'

'I love you, Daddy,' I repeated mechanically then raised my head slowly above his head, out of his sight, hoping he would not notice and mimed to negate what I had just said, 'I hate you.' Slowly, my lips came together and I was relieved he had not noticed.

It did not even occur to me that he was doing wrong. I simply loathed it. On Saturday afternoons he sometimes took me into his room for the same ritual. I had to stroke his private parts and he did the same to me. All the time the hatred grew. *If only the window cleaner would come. He could rescue me.* But there, as in the case of Rapunzel, there was no escape from the tower of terror. Years of hatred towards him were firmly embedded in my heart but, even so, the childhood love had never departed. It lay as the Dead Sea, trapped, unable to move, unable to grow, unable to express itself freely, innocently and trustingly towards the very person who was responsible for bringing me into this world. But instead of both him and other people being able to enjoy the buoyancy of my love, his and their debris rested on top and all around me like a garbage dump, 'You are the scum of the earth,' is how he spoke to us and, 'You killed Jesus.' But one thing touched me and I believed there was a glimmer of hope for our father when his favourite song came over the radio,
'Shh,'
We stood stock still. He walked over, crouched down, turned up the volume slightly and let the words seep into his lostness, 'I was Born Under a Wandering Star.' He only stood up when the entire song was finished; somebody was empathizing with him. A lost and lonely man, vulnerable to the universe, spent his time destroying the wandering stars that issued from him. We were becoming the black holes of humanity.

My father was not in the slightest interested in what went on for us at school. I knew no help would be offered for my homework so one day I put my intuition to the test. I dared to ask a question that would encourage some kind of interaction with me, other than abuse.

'Look it up,' he said, pointing to the three volumes of our red encyclopedias, 'and make sure you wash your hands first.'

I did not ask a second time. We held no conversations with him except when he was angry. No caring words crossed our ears. *I wish he was dead.* That was the only solution. There was no other way of getting free of that way of life. Secretly, I envisioned the police coming to tell us there had been an accident. One day they did come. My spirit rose as I opened the door to their hard knocking. One of them asked,

'Is your dad in?'

Oh. It's not about him. Huge disappointment hit every part of my being.

'No, my brother Alan is in charge. I'll go and get him for you.'

Alan went to the door. After a conversation out of my hearing he closed the door and on his return to the front room, explained,

'William has been arrested for stealing from the shop he's working in.'

'What was it?' I asked.

'Five pounds was found down his sock.'

Concern rose within me for William but I was not relieved with the news. Daddy was still alive and he would come home again that night. All was not over with him. Richard went to fetch William from the police station.

Peggy and Samantha, being unable to fully appreciate the burden on my shoulders, often sneaked out to play during school holidays and Saturdays. At those times I was left alone to work by myself. There was much to be done but as with any child there had to be play. In front of my father play was a barren field. I took the responsibility placed on me very seriously. The ability to foresee trouble coming was overdeveloped, causing me to become supersensitive to any wrong doing or supposed wrong doing. One Saturday Daddy came home, sat on the settee and told Samantha and I,

'I didn't see you at the park this afternoon.'

We had dared to ask him if we could go.

'Oh, no, we didn't go, we went to Blyster Park instead.'

'I didn't say I went to the park, I told you I didn't see you there.'

Nevertheless, such was our innocence of childhood destroyed that we felt it had been an accusation and not the intended joke.

The time came when I needed a break from the trauma. At fourteen years of age I longed for rest. More than anything I needed to be loved and cared for. The word love was never used in our house except when my father insisted I used it on him. One afternoon I put Samantha through a test. The tension between us had been strong and we had been arguing. I walked into the lounge and told her,

'I'm going to electrocute myself,' and headed for the kitchen.

She sat at the table in Daddy's place. I opened the tap. The sound of running water pouring into the bowl made a threatening noise.

'I'm wetting my hands now so the electricity will go straight through me and then I will die.' She did not answer. I carried on, 'I'm not drying them.' I came out into the hall and walked towards the front door, quickly pulled out the plug of the hoover along the skirting and said, 'Right, I'm doing it now.' She remained silent. I put my fingers to the side of the plug and slumped to the floor. Lying 'lifeless' for a while, still nobody came to the rescue and did not seem to care in the slightest. Then I heard a noise; Samantha was sobbing her heart out. She had sat at the table, folded her arms on it, pressed her aching head into them and sobbed. I stood up, 'It's okay, I'm really alive, I didn't do it. But now I know you love me.' At least I guessed she did.

One Saturday Daddy surprised some of us by saying he would take us to Berke's Buttons, a huge observatory in Lancashire. He did take us. We arrived safely, got out of the car and had a good look at the white satellite dishes from the surrounding fence. He took a photograph of us standing by the car and that was it, he drove us home again; nothing more to a rare day out with him. Another time and the only other time he took any of us for any leisure was to the swimming baths. He spent most of the time on his own swimming at the deep end. I could not swim and he came over for one minute to help me. I felt so awkward with his out of character attention that I could not do anything to make myself feel relaxed. He soon lost interest and went his way.

At home there were fights between brother and brother, brother and sister and sister and sister. Sometimes the result would be the victim being treated in casualty at Toy Town. One night, as I lay in bed, I heard a scuffling outside the front door. *What on earth is happening?* My heart beat fast as the voices of Richard and William rose up from the front doorstep. When boys fight, they fight and this was one that scared me a lot. I listened helplessly to muffled shouts and then silence. Glass smashed underneath the window of our room. I swallowed hard thinking somebody would be dead. It was not like my brothers to fight so roughly. Not even thinking to go down because we were not allowed out of bed once there, I fell asleep. Next morning William walked into our bedroom with slits for eyes. The smashed bottle was for him and Richard's pent up anger and frustration painted a nasty picture on his face. My helpless heart went out to both him and Richard. They were my brothers; orphans left to themselves in a desperate fight for life. William's badly bruised and swollen face smiled.

'You should go the Toy Town,' I said.

'No, I'll be alright.'

One night, after my bedtime, when Samantha was still awake and we were assured the boys were glued to the television we sneaked downstairs to steal a slice of dry bread. Our usual tea was two slices of bread and margarine after Daddy had finished his dinner. We were hungry by bedtime. The bread was counted daily but that did not stop our rumbling tummies. Sometimes we managed to put a bit of margarine on the bread. Usually, only one of us would go. That night both of us crept down to the kitchen, avoiding the creaky steps. After we silently took the bread from the wrapper and no stirrings from the front room were evident, we buttered it.

'Do you want a piggy back up the stairs? Don't make a noise,' I whispered to Samantha.

The slice of bread and margarine lay on top of her upturned hand. At the bottom of the stairs I crouched for her to get on. She put her right arm round my neck and climbed up onto my back. Her other hand carried the precious bread aloft. I reached three quarters of the way upstairs when mischief was afoot.

'I'm going to fall,' I teased, whispering.

Pretending to lose my footing I actually slipped. We crashed to the bottom of the stairs, landing on top of our umbrellas that lay against the wall. Samantha cried, got herself up and turned the corner to the toilet which was opposite the front door. As she sat there I recovered myself from the fall and looked upstairs.

'Sammy, look.'

'What?'

Laughing with all my might in a whisper I pointed up. She stuck her head out to see round the corner of the toilet.

'The bread, the bread, have you seen the bread?'

'I can't see it.'

'Yes, look, it's stuck to the wall.'

Her tears were instantly wiped away as she noticed the bread firmly clinging to the wallpaper above the banister. We should have thought to do the same. The sight of our vertical bedtime feast ruined our misery. We walked up the stairs and peeled the bread off. A dark, greasy mark remained and we prayed nobody would ever ask how it got there.

It was okay with Daddy if we were not cared for but if he was not cared for perfectly he made us pay. One night he woke me at midnight and told me to come downstairs,

'Why are those hankies still in the saucepan?'

He stirred them with a wooden spoon as they sat in a soft, cold paste. I had the routine job of boiling them for twenty minutes to kill off harmful bacteria.

'I forgot to rinse them.'

'Well, you can do them now and don't go to bed until you do.'

I lifted the large, heavy pan from the cooker, took it over to the sink, poured the slimy concoction into the washing up bowl and, for maybe an hour, slid one handkerchief over the other in clean water until they were back to normal. All the while thoughts of another nature brewed in my mind. I thought of our former escapes and wondered about another.

Alan and Richard have their own stories to tell of running away. Different ones of us ran away at different times. All we children wanted was to get out of home as fast as possible. William, Samantha and I had planned to run away *(when Peggy was still at Lincrest)*. One morning we took off. Having no sense of direction we guessed our way back to Kent. We had walked all day and it was getting dark and cold. William gathered up some brown paper that was lying around and, with the matches he brought with him, lit a fire in a bus shelter.

'This'll keep us warm,' he said, 'come on put your hands near it.' For two minutes that is exactly what we did as the fire quickly gobbled up the paper. In no time we were sitting around ashes. Sitting there for a few more minutes William, who was in charge, said, 'Come on, let's go.' We jumped up and made our way along the road. 'Hey, we can go into this field,' he said, 'over the fence we go.' In the dark we found a comfortable spot. However, we were not alone. As we felt around our hands rested on some warm, moist surfaces. 'Ah, cow's muck! We better get going again.' William showed his authority.

Samantha and I followed him out of the field and walked together feeling frightened and worried about what was going on at home.

'Do you think Alan and Richard will be getting into trouble cos we've gone?' I asked, 'I feel sorry for them but we had to get out of our house.'

'I think we better give up,' he said.

'Oh, we can't! We must be near Kent by now.' I could not imagine having to go home again to Daddy.

We approached a set of traffic lights and a lit up lamp on the wall of a police station attracted William more than it attracted me.

'We're going in to give ourselves up,' he announced.

'Oh no,' I grieved, then suddenly the brightest idea entered my thoughts, 'The police can get us to Kent!'

Here was the answer we were looking for.

'Where are we?' William asked after opening the door and standing before the straight faced police officer.

'This is Wigan.'

'But we should be in Wagonbridge, Kent,'

He took William aside. Samantha and I stood watching and waiting. The policeman disappeared and it was not long before a familiar looking gentleman walked in through the doors. My softness and compassion won me over as I approached him and gave my father a hug. Both that and my civil sounding father in his smart clothes had the police fooled into thinking everything was alright. We were returned home where any politeness shown in the police station completely vanished.

Some time later Samantha and I ran away on our own. I was twelve and Samantha nearly nine. We would get to Kent this time! On the morning of our planned escape, before anybody was awake, I slipped out of my bottom bunk and crept, in bare feet, past Daddy's bedroom to my brothers' bedroom. They were fast asleep. Alan's jacket lay at the bottom of his bed. I felt all through his pockets and found his wallet. Feeling sorry for him but also that we had no choice, I managed to extract ten pounds without waking him. I crept out of his room and back to my own bed. *My doll, I'll hide it up my doll's trouser leg.*

'Samantha, I've got the money. Remember, whatever you do, don't say anything. If we get to Kent then the others can come too.'

When Alan woke up he discovered his money missing, came into our room and asked,

'Has anybody taken ten pounds out of my wallet?'

'No.'

We yawned then turned over and, with faces straight and hearts set, closed our eyes. He said no more. I deeply regretted what I had done but it would serve well for all of us in the end. We would never normally do such a thing to our brother. He was a kind, quiet boy and never did anybody any harm. He always went to Mass and confession and took his religion seriously. The boys got Daddy up for work as we had asked for a rest from it and Samantha and I lay in bed pretending to be asleep. When William saw that we were not getting up for school he came into our room.

'Get up! You're going to be late.'

I remained asleep, just like he had years ago when I tried to wake him when Daddy wanted him. I kept my face as straight as a pole and breathed deeply. Samantha did the same on her top bunk. William was not bothered about her because she did not go to our school. When he got no response from me he reached into the bed, grabbed me underneath my arms and dragged me out. My pyjama trousers had a problem staying up but embarrassment refused to surface. I gave a quick tug with my hands behind my back but kept my eyes firmly shut. When he saw I was not about to wake up for anything he left. A few seconds later, to my relief, I heard the front door close. After everybody left the house, we did too - for good! I carried Pauline with me wrapped in my maroon and white pyjama trousers. We took nothing else but Alan's money, our accumulated dinner money and my school bus fare.

'Don't forget my name is Diana Bradwith and yours is Samantha Bradwith. If anybody asks us we are going back to our parents in Trinton, Kent. We have just been on holiday with the Pallitans, our cousins.' For the last time I put the key in the back door lock and turned it. The click sounded like a friend. 'Come on then,' I said, as Samantha took my hand. Once safely down the garden path and out of sight of our house there was no turning back. We caught the bus after walking the distance of the long avenue, about a mile, to the only place we knew – Centon, the place of our shopping. 'We have to ask somebody where the train station is. I'll ask this lady, she looks nice.' The tall, smartly dressed lady smiled as I politely and trustingly asked for directions,

'Excuse me, please can you tell us where the railway station is?'

'There's no station in Centon. The nearest one is Dillthorpe and you have to catch the bus to get there,' she told us, then walking away added, 'Stay where you are and I'll go and find out what number bus you want.'

I felt she could be trusted. We obediently awaited her return but she did not come back. It was not long before we realized we had been double-crossed. A police car pulled up and we were soon in it! They drove to a quieter place back the way we had come on the bus and stopped the car. The driver took Samantha out of the car and questioned her out of my hearing. The other, after returning and having conferred with the other one briefly, came over to me,

'What is your name?'

'Rachel Bradwith.'

'Your sister said your name is Diana Bradwith,' was his firm reply.

My brain was fresher than his and my response twice as firm.

'She must have been thinking about her cousin. She must be confused with all these questions.'

That was good enough for him; so far so good. Samantha did not get upset but acted calmly as they drove us to the station, Centon police station! We were led upstairs to a room on the left hand side of the building.

'Come in here and sit down,' invited the policeman.

We don't want to sit down. We sat regardless. Another policeman opened the door behind us bearing drawing paper and

loads of coloured pencils. We drew and coloured for what
seemed a year until questioned further,

'Where were you going?'

'To our home in Kent.'

'What's the address?'

'76 Peastring Lane, Trinton, Kent. We were trying to find the
railway station. We should be there by now,' I urged, mindless of
the fact that we had only left home about an hour before. Kent
was over two hundred and fifty miles away. 'They'll be leaving
to meet us soon. We have to hurry.'

I stared at my drawing then looked at Samantha's patterns.

'Just a minute!' He left the room. When he came back he said,
'Let me have your money.' I gave it to him. He counted every
penny. Looking at the other policeman sitting next to him he
declared, 'They have enough.' *Goody, goody. We can go now.* He
left the room again and on his return flattened my expectations,
stating,

'We've just sent a policeman round to Peastring Lane and he
said that Mrs Bradwith has told us all she knows about you.'

Oh what did she have to be in for? I had managed, with great
patience and the brilliant skill of a twelve year old to make the
police believe me. My hopes had soared as a happy future was
undoubtedly going to be ours. But after the betrayal from a
'trusted' lady we were not very happy little girls.

Back at school the following day the boys continued to scream
and run away whenever they saw me. I endured that, together
with Daddy's neglect and merciless behaviour, until I left both
school and home. My unhappiness turned into withdrawal to such
an extent that I hardly ever noticed other children in the school
and certainly had no quality friends. The only 'true' friend was
Edith because of my teacher's intervention. She was a good girl
and a very good Catholic. We often went home on the same bus
together, that is, before Peggy came home from Lincrest. As we
passed St Wilfred's church she lifted her hand to her forehead
and made the sign of the cross - I did not. She left a good
impression on me but our friendship came into question one day
when at an afternoon assembly in the main hall she was teased by
the boys who sat behind us. The soft canvas chairs were an
invitation for a sneaky foot to make contact with us. The boys got

up to their usual mischief but for a change, not with me. As usual we tried to ignore it but they were going for her; I was glad to get some respite from all the cruel goading. Eventually, being fed up with it, Edith turned around and said,

'If you don't stop you've got a fight after school.'

I was surprised at her change in character. Edith was usually quiet and not at all aggressive. The boy in question, Gerald, did not listen. He gave another kick, at which, Edith turned around a second time and said, 'Right, you've got a fight after school!'

After the session Gerald reminded her,

'Don't forget we've got a fight later.'

She turned and stated quite emphatically,

'Rachel's having it for me.'

I stared at her in utter shock. My anger too had had enough static reactions for a lifetime so I took advantage of the situation and especially as he was smaller than us,

'Okay, I will.'

After school crowds of children were waiting for a different fight. I, like a bull; horns and hoof ready for war planted my satchel on an unsuspecting Edith. I removed Gerald's glasses politely and laid into him with all my might. I dragged his bottom lip up to his left ear stretching it mightily, pulled his short hair and punched him. My anger still was not finished when he hit me in the face. No way would I allow that, it was not worth it. The thought of being scarred for life made me walk away. Gerald did not follow so I reckon he had had enough too. Next morning, Edith and I were taken before Mrs Wayne, the head mistress.

'Were you two fighting outside the school last night?'

'Well, I was but it was Edith's fight. Gerald was kicking her under her chair and wouldn't stop.'

'Right, no excuses, girls should not fight. You can choose six of the best with the strap, or five hundred lines?'

I had enough beatings at home but let Edith decide,

'I'll take the lines,' she said.

'As a girl I must not fight,' instructed Mrs Wayne. Gerald chose the strap. I felt the entire situation was grossly unfair.

During the Easter holiday in my third year I wanted to ask Daddy for a school tie. I knew he would say no but the desire to ask him never left me. I pondered the question for six months and often discussed the matter with Peggy and Samantha.

'Why don't you ask when Mrs Fabican's here?' suggested Samantha.

So next time Mrs Fabican came I asked him,

'Daddy, is it alright if I have a school tie?'

'Yes, how much are they?' he asked and after I told him he gave me the money.

Mrs Fabican never knew anything bad about our father. He had met her when we lived in Kent through a Catholic paper of some sort and that is why he moved up to Cheshire; to be near her. We presumed that when he went out every evening it was to be with her but he really could have been going anywhere. He never told us.

Being as good as locked up on the inside emotionally, unable to express or receive any true love and affection I became unable to function as a human being. Without encouragement or praise we drifted through life from day to day. My tolerance had been phenomenal and it was time to push at the prison walls to see if they would give way. When Mrs Barkson, my next door neighbour, asked one day,

'Would you like to do some babysitting for us? We'll pay you,' the thought of earning a little bit of money was a great temptation.

'Yes, I'll do it,' I said confidently, hiding my misgivings.

'Be sure to ask your dad,' she said.

I did ask and, as anticipated, he said no. However, no was not good enough for me and I was not doing anything wrong. I would go and take the risk. William backed me up,

'Tell Dad you went to Doris Partly's.'

Doris, who was a friend to us children, though had little to do with us, lived only a block away and was five years older than me.

The first night went fairly smoothly. William left the catch on the front door. I came home after a successful evening, pushed the door and released the catch to lock it then sneaked upstairs, striding over the top three creaky ones and after a quick wash got into bed. It was all so easy. The following night, as I had not grasped how to release the catch quietly, it made a loud click as I pushed the button upwards. Unlike last night Daddy was in, which was rare indeed. I could hear his voice from behind the closed front room door which kept the heat from the fire in the room. Quickly, I took my shoes off and was three quarters of the way up the stairs when the front room door opened. I stood absolutely still knowing that if I dashed, albeit like a fairy, the stairs at the top would give me away. I stood as though a lion was about to seize me by the throat. My heart beat shock waves through my body. I was caught, nowhere to run. My body lost all strength as I went limp inside. Daddy walked up the hall, looked at the door, turned and saw me.

'Come down!' I knew it was time to be beaten up. 'Where have you been?'

'At Doris's.'

William kept his word saying,

'Yes, she was at Doris's.'

I had already put Doris in the picture in case Daddy asked her. I think the whole of Hockbury was afraid of Daddy. I got away without a beating and so from then on naturally it would be easy to earn some money for myself. I knew never to treat the lock that way again and so was bound to be able to babysit for many months to come. The following night, armed for success, I left for the five or six steps journey to next door. Peggy and Samantha followed,

'You can't come. We'll all get caught and battered,' I warned.

They would not hear my desperate pleas for them to stay at home. Perhaps they were afraid to be left at home, I did not know. So there we were, three of us babysitting when suddenly our ears pricked up as we heard a knock at the front door. Richard's voice shouted through the letter box,

'You have to come home.'

He had seen my hair. Samantha and I urged Peggy,

'Go home and say it was you. That way you won't get into trouble.'

'No, I'm not going,' she demanded adamantly.

Terror pulsed through our bodies. The Barkson children were also very much afraid. What were we to do? Peggy went home eventually to say I was not at the Barkson's. No one knew about Samantha being with me. From then on Samantha and I, nor the

Barkson's, would answer the door because we were not there. Not wanting to be seen from outside we crawled around on our hands and knees. Three year old Shelley Barkson urged me,

'Hide behind the chair. Take your jumper off.'

I did so, not because she was right to leave my white blouse glowing in the dark but because of her caring little heart. It seemed all our neighbours gathered at the windows front and back to get us out, including the Frenick family who lived a few blocks away and who were our enemies. We stayed where we were, unable to do the job required of us. The children we were babysitting acted as high security officers. Nine o'clock came and they were still up. I was hoping it would be all over by the time Mr and Mrs Barkson returned. The neighbours eventually gave up and went away but we dared not relax. Suddenly, there was another knock on the front door. A gruff voice shouted through the letter box,

'Come out now!'

Samantha crept to the kitchen window on her hands and knees to see who it was. I hovered out of sight in the hall.

'It's Daddy!' she whispered, turning pale.

We remained silent. Daddy went away and then out for his evening later than usual.

Mr and Mrs Barkson eventually arrived back and they very much sympathized with us. Mrs Barkson said,

'You can't stay here for the night. Tell your dad I forced you to babysit,' trying to save our skins, 'if he asks me I'll say that.'

Richard came again and shouted through the letter box,

'If you come home, get ready for bed, put your dressing gown on and go to sleep I'll wake you up when Dad gets home. I'll do my best to protect you.'

With that reassurance I went home with him but knew there was no escaping what was to come. Samantha also came but Daddy knew nothing of her being with me. She was okay. I thanked the Barkson's. At midnight I was woken up by Richard. How I slept I will never know. I followed him downstairs where Daddy demanded,

'Why did you go next door when I told you not to?'

'Mrs Barkson forced me to,' I answered, thankful to her.

That was not a good enough excuse. He turned to Richard,

'Go and get Peggy and Samantha down here.'

On their arrival Daddy smacked me round the head a few times. Peggy watched. I saw her pained face. As I stood with my back to the sofa and my father standing between Peggy and myself, I thought, *this night it will be different.* I no longer wanted to defend myself. I let him hit and hit me opened faced. My body was his to do all he wanted with. My brothers and sisters stood by. We had done so since we were very small and knew no different. He was the final answer to everything. Daddy walked around the room, shouting and backing me towards the armchairs that sat side by side against the wall that divided the lounge from the kitchen. Their two inner arms made a seat on this occasion. I did not resist him. My hearing had already partially gone because of the punches to the side of my head. As I landed on the chair arms Daddy grabbed hold of my legs and pushed my knees into my eyes. I think he may have killed me that night. He did not notice that I let him help himself to his spleen against me and then he suddenly stopped.

'I'm going round to ask Mrs Barkson if she forced you to go round there.'

I had no fear of that. Our agreement had been made but I wondered what she would say. Would she keep her word? He marched out of the front room and down the hall leaving the doors wide open. I listened for his knocks. The silence was almost tangible. My urge to escape through the open front door became more desperate. In my mind I ran all the way, in my dressing gown, to the Catholic Church; running wildly through the streets, away down the cinder path and arriving at the Priest's house approximately one and a half miles away. Fear brought me back to reality. My feet stuck fast to the carpet, unwilling to meet Daddy on his return. Mrs Barkson's television only grew louder with each of his knocks resulting in his furious temper increasing and endangering me even more. I felt betrayed but reckon she was as scared as I was. *Why did she not call the police?* She must have heard the rage coming from him. We heard the door close as he walked back into the house and his ever closer footsteps kept me frozen.

'She's not answering,' he announced on reentering the front room.

I expected him to release more rage because of that but instead he calmed. Whatever was going on in his head I will never know. He sent me to bed.

Next morning I was still deaf. My body was cold and shivering, reacting from the shock of the onslaught. My ears and tops of my arms were black and blue, so were my heart and soul. That time I had something to show them at school and maybe it would bring the rescue we so longed for. When I arrived tears were not far away. Edith wanted to know what was wrong so I showed her my injuries and she took me to the headmistress,

'Take her to the medical room, please,' said Mrs Wayne.

I was still trembling. What was left of any dignity was stripped away. The nurse from the medical room sent me to the school clinic. There, the nurse examined my ear. Her mouth almost cupped over the top of it as she peered in using her thin torch,

'What happened to you?'

'My dad hit me.'

'Oh, have you been a naughty girl then?' she sneered.

'No.'

'The wax is dislodged. I'll have to syringe it.'

Nothing further was done. It seemed nobody cared at all. So life at home carried on as usual.

Every Saturday Samantha and I went shopping with two pounds in cash to feed six of us for the week. Oh, of course, Daddy, for want of a more appropriate name, as it certainly was not a term of endearment, made seven. Alan used to do the shopping and had taken me with him a few times so I learned what to do. Doris helped me through the first signs of womanhood when I had no idea what to do on my first period. I would have been stuck without her and did not know where the money would come from for my new need. I had to sneak an additional item onto the shopping list. My father never explained nor found anybody to help me for the change in my physical or otherwise growing up stage.

After shopping one day I ironed Daddy's shirts perfectly as required and hung them on the back of a chair for him to take upstairs then sat down on the same chair for a rest. He unexpectedly walked into the front room from upstairs and caught me leaning against the shirts. Without a word he yanked me by my left arm over the back of the chair which broke with the force.

The following weekend Mother Bede, our ex Child Care Officer, took us girls to her offices in Wigan, as arranged by our father. There was a games room at the bottom of the garden with a huge rocking horse amongst the other toys. When left to ourselves we took turns swinging on the horse backwards, forwards, then backwards and forwards again with the intention of flying through the closed door and off into infinity, in other words playing too hard. Whilst lost in this new freedom, we suddenly heard footsteps advancing towards the door. In an instant we leapt to our feet whilst rendering everything motionless and pushing hard against the horse's head and neck to bring it to a sudden stop. Samantha had dismounted while it was still in wild motion. It was as though a boomerang had been thrown. Totally expressionless and in absolute silence the three of us faced the door statue like and braced ourselves for an onslaught of anger. The door opened and we were caught doing absolutely nothing, just as we had been trained to do. A huge mountain of guilt hid behind our wide eyed veneers as two nuns walked in. There was no sign of anger as anticipated and it was not too long before Mother Bede drove us home. She knew about our home situation but still there was no rescue. We were not allowed to play and have fun. Daddy always demanded an explanation for a smile. Happiness was a crime and most definitely banned.

For a few weeks Daddy gave me half a crown pocket money but that stopped when I became ill one week and had to stay at home from school. I was left with nothing so with his permission I got a paper round. I hated it and did not last very long after encountering a ferocious dog. Instead of posting the paper I threw it hurriedly over the garden gate and that was that. The following attempt at obtaining some money was made at the corner of our maisonettes in a public telephone box. William took Samantha and me in there with him one day. We watched as he put a lolly stick from his pocket up the slot where change came out, wiggled it a bit and out popped shillings, sixpences, and threepences. A few days later I thought I would have a go and have some money at last. A whole lot of coins rushed out to greet my stick. William was not far away and heard the excited jingling sound. He had never got as much as that.

'What are you doing?' I heard his angry voice behind me, 'If you don't put all that back I'll phone the police.'

I needed no more threat. Immediately the whole lot reluctantly went back where it came from. It took quite a bit of time getting so much back with the stick. I could only manage one coin at a time. Out I came and in he went – got the lot. I believed him, why shouldn't I? He was my brother. Then one day after school he told me,

'Trevor Onsort has got a bike for you.'

'Where?'

'He's making it. Just give us your bus fare and you'll have it soon.'

'Yeah, but I'll have to walk all that way and back every day.'

'Well, that's okay. You'll have a bike soon.'

'Okay.'

My very own bike! For a few weeks I walked to school trusting my bike was nearing completion and deciding I had waited long enough, I asked,

'Where is it William, where's my bike?'

'Trevor's just getting the handle bars on. Tell you what, give us your dinner money too and it'll be done quicker.'

I gave him my two shillings and sixpence plus my bus fare. In class my teacher wanted to know where my dinner money was or I could not have dinner.

'My brother's got it.'

'Well, go and ask him for it.'

'Do I have to?'

'Go and ask him for your dinner money.'

I left the room. I had enough trouble facing my own class but then had to face his class full of strangers. With every step towards his classroom my shoulders scrunched into my neck. My teacher was not there to protect me. He wanted his money. I knocked on William's classroom door.

'Come in,' shouted the teacher.

I opened the door and asked to speak to William. Thankfully, he was sitting at the front.

'Where's my dinner money?'

'I haven't got it?'

'My teacher wants it or I can't have any dinner.'

'I haven't got it.'

'Well, where is it?'

'I've spent it.'

'What on?'

'Jammie dodgers.'

'You mean all these weeks you've been spending my money on jammie dodgers? Well, where's my bike?'

'Peter, the guy who was getting all the parts for Trevor is moving to Scotland.'

'Yeah, you weren't making it all along, were you?'

He looked at me with upturned eyes and head down as I stood before the class. I always trusted everything people told me.

When Peggy had returned home from Lincrest a year after I did she joined me at St Peter's. During her second winter at home the snow fell heavily, blanketing the way to school. We reached the bus stop at the top end of the cinder path. The bus was late.

'Shall we just go home again?' asked Peggy.

'No, we'd better go to school; we've been off too much already.'

'The bus is late. Let's get some sweets,' I suggested.

We turned around and trudged to the corner shop.

'Better hurry up,' I said as I opened the door to come out. Peggy followed. I looked behind to make sure she was there. Her face was aghast. 'What are you looking at?' I asked.

Turning to where Peggy was looking straight ahead of me, through the door window, a helpless post woman lay face up on the snow. Her round body resembled a huge football with arms and legs and, without hope of getting up as she bounced around, buffeted gently on all sides with her postbag firmly attached to her arm. Nobody would be able to prize that off her.

'Let's help her up,' suggested Peggy. So like Sherlock Holmes and Doctor Watson we peered over her. Peggy, being wonderful with people, chatted away with her as she lay freezing on the ground, 'Can we lift you up?' She offered while stretching towards her.

We grabbed an arm each and tried to pull her to her feet. Her weight and shape did not help at all. She slid around this way and that, her bag complimenting every move. We could take no more and burst out laughing. With sides hurting, knees giving way and strength gone, we were useless.

'I'm sorry,' I managed to say, 'I can't help you.'

She joined us with a laugh that made us laugh all the more.

'Try to put your knees up. We'll try to help you,' persisted Peggy.

But it was no use, the situation had reached the hysterical stage. She desperately tried to raise one leg but her laughter made her too weak to help herself.

'We're going to be late for school,' I said, concerned that it would take another hour or two to get her to her feet. Still laughing she said,

'You better leave me till the snow melts.'

We all laughed again till tears rolled down our cheeks. Peggy and I continued to laugh as we walked away waving goodbye.

'We'll check to see if you've managed when we get back from school.'

'I'll manage to get up.'

She lay there laughing, as far as we were concerned, all day long.

Due to the neglect and cruelty of our father there was quite a bit of savagery in our family. Our hearts were good but the seed of God that was placed in us when we were born was not nurtured the way it should have been. There was no sign of the neglect and cruelty ending in the future either. All I knew was that I had to stay at home until old enough to leave. After that there would be no more problems. The frustration was continually on the surface. It seems like all our fights rolled into one eternal family war with scattered peace here and there. Peggy and I were arguing one day and as I stormed into the kitchen she followed and her finger happened to be between the doorpost and the hinges of the door but I was unaware of it and slammed the door shut. Her finger was a horrible sight for a long time afterwards.

Another day Peggy and I were fighting. She had a real will of her own and my anger often got the better of me. We were both upstairs and as she ran downstairs I leaned over the banister and grabbed; her hair landed in my clenched fist but she carried on running down the stairs rather like a cartoon cat when there's nothing to run on. After I let go she pulled handfuls of hair out of her head. The banister was high and I certainly did not expect the results of my actions to produce such a scene. The following Saturday afternoon while we were in the kitchen doing the washing and other chores, Richard interrogated Peggy about something, he lifted her off the floor by the hair and in marched 'Jonas' *(a nickname my brothers had for Daddy, though he never knew).* For him to have been horrified was a miracle in itself. He did the same to Richard. No-one in my family knew what it was to be loved; there was no room for it. At the age we were we did not think of what we were doing, we just did it. Day blended into day and we disjointedly drifted along as best we could. What happened to the love and unity of our family that I had so longed for as a child?

William did whatever he pleased many times and adopted an old man's dog from across the road. Bouncer was quite old but great fun. William dressed him up every summer in a football outfit. He, Bouncer, never lived with us and we did not know his owner. On Saturdays on route to do our shopping he came with us all the way to the bus stop along the long avenue and waited there patiently for our return. On one occasion he followed me two miles to the doctor's surgery. I felt scruffy in my tatty old brown anorak and navy skirt. As I sat in the waiting room in marched Bouncer and sniffed out everybody. In embarrassment I ignored him. In front of people I could not have anything. I sensed Daddy's thoughts, commandments and attitudes of disapproval oozing out of the faces I could not even raise my head to look at. My father had pushed me right into myself where people were concerned.

'You shouldn't have that dog,' they snarled.

I pretended I did not know Bouncer at all and thankfully he did not recognize my scent so left the surgery.

Nobody was Daddy's favourite. He showed none of us any respect nor gave us time to just enjoy him and he kept a keen eye on his food cupboard in the front room. The sideboard near the window held his biscuits and cakes. We had none. It was his cupboard and we were not supposed to touch it. When he was not about we opened the door and found a way of taking some then hiding the evidence. One evening Daddy came home and discovered somebody had been at the cakes. All of us were held to account.

'William, have you been touching my cakes?' he shouted.

Without giving him a chance to answer he removed a Madeira cake from the cupboard, partially unwrapped it then pushed the entire cake into William's face. The rest of us stood in silent anxiety wondering what would happen next. While continuing to shout angrily he threw his own beans on toast straight onto the fire.

William eventually got a job with the baker who brought bread and cakes around the neighbourhood in a van. For a long time he worked on that van but one day a hefty bill came through the door. Alan questioned William as to how it could be so high and whilst doing so grabbed his shirt front and lifted him up the wall. Poor William had to confess he had been taking cakes and putting them on the bill but he had hidden them in Blyster Park. He took me to his den there one time and I saw the hoard with my own eyes but, except for a large slice of Battenberg cake, was not allowed any of the mouth watering goodies.

A few days after the questioning of William, Samantha and I were fighting. The kitchen was the scene of battle where Samantha slammed the door not realizing Peggy's finger was again on the other side of it. As it slammed shut Peggy's unsuspecting finger was crushed in line with the hinges and she needed hospital treatment. She had a habit of putting them there. We ran away again after that. Our destination was Kent as usual. Again, however, we ended up going north but because we travelled in a different direction to the other times, it must be the right one - South. Our arrival that time was the Pennines, a beautiful hilly area of English countryside. We were a great distance from home but somehow made our way back before Daddy got home from work.

Some of our truancy days were spent at home. We bought 'lucky numbers' sweets. None of which proved to be lucky. On one such occasion the three of us girls decided we would like to play with Daddy's tape recorder. There were no instructions so we used it by instinct. It was great fun to hear our voices come through loud and clear. Daddy would never know we touched it because we learned how to rub the evidence off, leaving it 'untouched'. We loved it so much so played with it often.

Our fights were not always unpleasant and on our truant days smarty fights were rarely missing, throwing them in the air at each other and catching them in our mouths if we could. We were always much better when the three of us girls were left to ourselves with no pressure. In between the tape recorder antics and the smarty fights something went wrong one time without our notice and so we carried on as normal and went to bed as usual. Little did we know that another midnight nightmare was about to begin. Richard got us all up and once downstairs we were interrogated by Daddy,

'Who's been playing with the tape recorder?'

'Not me,' we chimed together.

'Well, what was the cushion doing on the floor?'

'Oh, we were playing with it.'

'Playing with the cushion? Well, what was the lid doing off my tape recorder?'

'We don't know.'

'Richard, get something to hit them with,' he demanded. 'Get the poker.'

Richard had made the iron poker in metalwork at school. He stared at Daddy in disbelief and was terrified at what he had been told to do. We still did not own up to using the machine because Daddy was not one to relent on punishment. When he realized Richard was not about to use the poker on his sisters, he took it out of his hand,

'Right, bend over the couch. Samantha?'

Obediently she took the first hit. Peggy was next and myself last. Daddy did not spare the strength of his strikes against his daughters. On the third round Peggy decided that Samantha had had enough,

'I did it,' she bravely volunteered.

Her admission took me by surprise. It was not any one person's fault. It was all three of us but Daddy's persistence would have gone on all night and the punishment would have increased and become more severe with every round.

'Go out of the room!' he ordered William, Samantha and me.

We stood outside the door and listened as Daddy kept hitting Peggy with the poker. I was really frightened for her. When he eventually finished with her she was black and blue. She could not sit or lie down for a week nor did she know what made him stop so suddenly and offer her an egg flip. He made her drink the horrible stuff. After that we were more than determined to get out of our home and to take the poker as proof with us. When Peggy was able to walk properly again we got ourselves ready for yet another journey down south,

'We have to put loads of clothes on,' I instructed. 'We can't take any bags or we'll get caught.'

So dressing in all the clothes we thought we would need; two or three layers at least, we were prepared never to return. Even though it was the hottest of days we had to take it all. We never used public transport when running away to avoid being reported for wagging school, plus the fact that we had very little money. By midday we were in a strange place. We made our way to a huge green which was a lovely spot to have some lunch. I walked a great distance across the green to a small shop keeping an eye out for signs of police cars, Daddy or my brothers who might turn up and take us home again. None of us felt safe for one minute. I made it to the shop without incident and bought a packet of biscuits and other things to eat. We were determined not to be caught again. After a rest we got going in case somebody might find us if we stayed too long. We continued with our poker to Kent. After walking all day we settled to spend the first night in a bus shelter and would start again in the morning.

'I'm sure they won't be able to find us. How will they know where we are?' I reassured the three of us.

Peggy kept messing about though, crawling around on all fours and thrusting her leg into the air,

'There's a police car coming,' she teased while sticking her leg out of the shelter.

Then the sound of a car approaching made her put her leg back inside double quick. It was indeed a police car and it stopped – nowhere to hide, my heart sank. Peggy had not meant to be seen. We would never get away. It had taken us hours to get there and again we gave the story about Kent. We were soon in the policeman's car and being taken for a ride.

'Are we near Wagonbridge?' I asked the officer.

'No, this is Lower Trosburgh,'

We were farther up north as usual. Would we never learn to go in the opposite direction? The well built law officer drove us to his house and I will never forget him. He was the kindest man I had ever met. It was eleven o'clock at night. Inside his beautiful house his wife made us a meal of ham and baked beans. It was the best meal we had tasted for as long as we could remember; not because it was beans and ham but that it was made by a caring, loving mother figure and that we felt perfectly safe there. We pleaded with them not to send us back home and showed them the poker. It felt really good to be in the company of what I would call a real mum and dad. Daddy finally arrived to claim his tearaways and was told about the wonderful meal we had eaten. Why could adults not use some wisdom when dealing with children in distress? Daddy never touched us that night.

Not many evenings later Peggy and I arrived home from school where I reached into my skirt pocket as usual for the back door key.

'My key!' I shouted, 'Where's the key?'

'It must be at school,' Peggy suggested.

'It must be. Now we've got to go all the way back to find it. What are we going to say to Daddy?'

'I don't know.'

We walked back to school and searched all the classrooms I had been in during the day. We cried but the caretaker did not see the matter as serious,

'It's no good crying over spilt milk,' he said as he led us from classroom to classroom. It was hardly milk. After an hour I found the key in one of the classrooms. It must have fallen out of my pocket and onto the floor. By that time it was six o'clock. 'Do you like at home?' he asked without a care in the world, even though he was a caretaker.

'No,' we replied emphatically.

'Well, go home and like.'

It was two years before the penny dropped and I understood what he had actually meant. From that day I tied the key to my skirt buttonhole with a piece of string. I do not recall the aftermath to that episode.

I so yearned for our mother to come back. My hope was that if I wrote to her maybe she would come back. I had to try. So after writing my heart rending plea I took the letter over to the fireplace and set light to it. As I watched the edges turn red with the heat, then black and then grey my heart filled with hope. With the same poker that had travelled to Lower Trosburgh with us I lifted my freshly burned paper and sent it up the chimney, then dashed outside to make sure it was soaring up toward Heaven. I believed she would get it and reply. Nearly every day I suggested to my sisters,

'Wouldn't it be great if, when we come home from school, all the work is done, fire lit, tea ready and Mummy is back.'

I dreamed, dreamed and dreamed, then, one day my dream came true. Peggy and I returned home from school and walked down the garden path towards the back door. Looking in the front room window, before putting the key in the lock, I saw and my heart pounded. All the work was done and the fire prepared. Dare I go in? Had she really been in Australia? Did she just go away and not want to come back? Had she received my letter? I was scared, to say the least and half excited. Was she in the kitchen getting tea ready? I unlocked the door and walked inside, Peggy followed. I thought that as we had at least got that far with the noise we made somebody would have come to see who had walked in but all was quiet. So where was Mummy? Where could she be? Nowhere, that's where. Again it was a massive disappointment and all was a mystery as to who had done the work. I found out later that it was Mrs Fabican but was that just an assumption?. My hopes of having a mother were almost realized. We were grateful to Mrs Fabican but why had she not stayed to welcome us or even left a note and how did she know how to prepare the fire? Nobody was ever in when Peggy and I returned from school. There was simply no mum. That was the only day the work was done for us.

While dusting the following week it occurred to me that Daddy never showed us what was in his cupboards so I took it upon myself to take a look. We only knew what was in his food cupboard in the sideboard but I felt it was time for us to know what was in the rest of it and what was in a huge trunk in his bedroom. After all we were his children, why shouldn't we know? Opening one of the drawers in the sideboard I took out an old Kent newspaper. The headline in big bold print read: 'Mother of Six Dies'. I read the article with great interest. There it was - so she was not in Australia; neither did our dog go looking for her. She died when she was thrown from the back of Daddy's motor scooter while he was bringing her back from work. It had got a puncture and the temporary repair had not worked. The rear wheel came loose. She looked around when the scooter started to wobble and shouted,

'Oh, Jonathan!'

She was flung off and her skull was fractured as soon as her head hit the road. She died later that evening in Kent General Hospital. Her preference when riding the scooter was never to wear a crash helmet and the consequences of that freedom fell upon us all and probably the last thing she would have wanted was the terrible suffering and upheaval that ensued.

Next, I took hold of the photograph album; I wanted to know what we all looked like when we were small and what our mother looked like. I opened the hard cover and then the translucent sheet that protected the images. Many photographs of my brothers, grandparents, aunties, uncles, cousins and people I did not know were there too and there, included in them all was our mother; she was so beautiful, except her eyes; one was different from the other. So that is where I got my bad eyesight from! In that black and white photograph she was only eighteen years old. Her dark hair, which was really auburn, was swept back from her forehead and she was wearing a white overall but only the top bit was showing. She had touched us, as shown in a photograph of Peggy sitting on her lap and her hand lay gently across Peggy's head, so tenderly, so motherly. Another one showed her giving Peggy and me an ice lolly. Peggy, wearing her nappy, stood not knowing what to do with it; another one of us three girls in the back garden playing with the newspaper. I did not expect to look the way I did as a young infant with my short curly hair. There was a family photograph of us sitting around a table outside with some other people; it was not our home but a bit like a cafe. Daddy was standing behind the boys who were sitting at the other side of the table. My legs looked quite uncomfortable as I stood in front of my mother. Her hand was across my tummy, holding me. If only I could remember that touch. I must have been almost two years old. Peggy was sitting on Mummy's lap. Samantha was not yet born. I continued to thumb through the album with my sisters. There were many Naval war photographs where our father wore his sailor's outfits aboard ships and other snapshots of what went on when he was on the war vessels, including one of a bear cub rolling on deck playing with the lads. The emptiness and sadness of who was missing from our lives was almost too much to cope with. When finished I closed the album slowly but reluctantly.

Turning my attention to the trunk in Daddy's bedroom, I asked, 'Shall we open it?' but did not wait for an answer.

The lid, I was happy to discover, was not locked. Inside, I found lots of things that belonged to our mother. There were different coloured skeins of wool, lots of music sheets and a piano book with the words, 'To Felicity, on your fourth birthday.' It was worn and old but still intact. I leafed through the pages carefully. The music sheets were far too hard for any of us to understand. Perhaps there were other things in there that I do not recall and when finished scouring through to the very bottom we put everything back the way we found it. One item we pulled out was a white pleated tennis skirt. My mother was slim; I wondered how she fitted into it. Some time after discovering all those things Daddy went through the trunk and gave me that skirt. He must have known what we had been up to and decided to say nothing. As for the wool, my sisters and I spent many hours winding one skein after the other into huge balls. They were left over from the knitting machine that was no longer anywhere to be seen. After looking in the trunk I remembered the presents I was not allowed to have and got a chair to look on top of his wardrobe. They were still there but I dared not take them down. Whilst on the chair my eyes caught sight of something that shocked me; the betrayal, the meanness of our father was hidden up there. Not concealed, not covered up but away from our spotting it, was a wad of banknotes which I counted - £600. All that money and I could not have a school uniform, we could not eat properly, we were taken nowhere, we were not bought any clothes. It was money saved to buy a car for Mrs Fabican. That night I asked for the presents but did not say what we had been up to. He let me have them at last and perhaps that is what prompted him to look through the trunk. I was satisfied that at least some long standing questions had been answered and we got to see what our mother was like all those years ago. I wondered what she would be like now.

Both day and night there was trouble and Peggy still wet the bed during her sleep because of stress. Aunty Jean used a buzzer when we lived with her and everybody heard it when it went off as it alerted Peggy she needed the toilet. I think it was done away with after it failed to do its job properly and to save Peggy the ongoing embarrassment. Not only did she suffer the shame but also had to endure bitter punishment from Daddy. One Saturday morning he made her and William carry her ruined stained mattress through the streets to the dump. Her previous punishment was that she had to hang it over the washing line in the back garden. Our mattresses were only about one and a half inches thick with grey and white stripes. After her mattress was gone she was left with nothing but newspaper and polythene on the floor, plus a draw sheet. Night after night she lay like that. She had no night clothes, just Daddy's unwanted vest to wear. Every morning she was soaked and very comfortable in the warmth that clung to her but always the dreaded moment came, either Samantha or I suddenly, with a swift yank, pulled the covers away. We were not being cruel; it was an understanding that, if we had not, she would have stayed there forever and Peggy was both brave and grateful. She never pulled the covers back over because the coldness of the air stuck to the wet sheets. She washed her bedding as soon as she was up, under Daddy's orders. At one point Daddy brought an upright armchair and made her sleep in that. How could anybody sleep sitting up all night?

The lack of love and security and the violent tension affected us in different ways. As a result of neglect Peggy's long red hair 'went to pot'. She had not washed it for many months. It did not look dirty so nobody forced her to wash it. At one of our regular visits to the school clinic the nurse washed Peggy's hair. It must have been the longest single job she ever encountered. We watched as the nurse rinsed away the freshly washed dirt from Peggy's head at least twenty eight times before it came clean. We did laugh but I was amazed that her hair had not given the slightest impression it was dirty at all. It was the same colour after it was washed as it had been before. But again, we were sent back home. How did our father get away with such neglect?

Peggy needed a tooth out at the clinic one afternoon. I went with her and sat in the waiting room which was full of mothers waiting for their children. Being motherless was thrust in my face yet again and I also did not like the thought of the blood that would follow once her tooth was gone and so when the nurse came and asked,

'Would you like to come through to your sister?'

'No,' was my quick response and one that I thought was expected of me.

Not that I did not care for my sister. I did care and felt her pain. I simply thought she would come out when she was ready and was I not already there waiting for her? I discovered very quickly that her question was not an invitation but an order. I was fed up with being a child and thought that once I grew up adults would not bother me and that only children got told off so I looked forward to getting out of my childhood years. All the trouble in my life would end.

During the summer holidays we carried on working at home and went out to play on occasions. We never went anywhere abroad or even to the seaside like normal families. As early as eight in the mornings as soon as Daddy left for work we girls were out playing airplanes with folded newspapers on the green opposite or throwing a ball against the side of the maisonettes. On occasions a girl from Samantha's school invited us to the local old folk's home to ask the old people if they wanted shopping done. That way we would get some money and perhaps sweets.

At the end of the holidays I dreaded the newness of a fresh school year. At the beginning of every term the pupils in class voted for a form leader. I was never chosen but in the third year the boys surprised me. However, they soon learned that I was not that much of a fool. It was an ideal opportunity to show them that I was made of more than just a red face. They thought they would have an easy ride but that had not been my intention at all. I carried out my duties every day; collecting the register, taking it to the teacher's desk and returning it to the office when she finished with it. I had learned to handle responsibility well but mixing with people became harder and harder. When the tutor was out of the room I stood at the front of the class to report any bad behaviour. The blackboard was never short of initials; mostly boys. Every time they spoke, my fingers, which held the chalk, quickly scribbled their identification. I never backed off, being a bag of subdued anger. One peep out of any or them was enough to condemn them. I do not remember the teachers ever taking any notice of what was on the board. With every initial placed I felt my face burn. Inferiority spread all over it. To be the only girl that went red was such a handicap but when one girl, Olivia, a girl I admired for her confidence and maturity spoke, her words helped boost my morale slightly,

'You are doing very well but don't keep going red; you spoil it,' said Olivia, in front of the whole class.

I took the remark as a compliment, realizing that without such a problem I would have gained a lot of respect. Not knowing why my face got hot and red I went to the doctor. In his office I explained the problem and he listened sympathetically but must have been screaming with laughter on the inside. He started to write on a piece of paper and, when finished, handed it to me,

'Take this and it should stop.'

I left his office, took the prescription to the chemist and emerged with the pink medicine, confident that it would be just what I needed. It did not cure anything and I continued to 'blush' as the doctor called it. I understood then what William had said way back. How I tolerated or found the strength to cope with the problems, only God knows. Then, to test me even further, I was leaning against the wall of the gym alone one Wednesday afternoon playtime. The expanse of the playground lay open before me with fewer children than usual. Something strange was happening. As I looked around I noticed only girls were playing, mostly on the playing field and a scattering of them in the playground. All the boys were gathered in the far playground that was surrounded by fencing. We called it the pen. *I know what they're doing.* I stood, watched and waited. As the group swelled I stayed exactly where I was. They were going to do something to me! There were approximately two hundred and fifty of them. A little while later the bulk started to walk out of the pen and across the playground in my direction. They marched to within ten inches, staring and chanting my name. Suddenly, I kicked out towards them, at which, they about turned and fled. A few weeks later I tried a bit of bullying myself and picked on a timid looking lad. The remorse I felt later became too strong and I never did it again. Two questions have remained with me over the years and that is, why do people do it? How did they concoct such an ingenious plan behind my back? I never hurt anyone with such malice but was continually getting bombarded with cruelty and neglect.

Despite the problems I did well in some of the lessons; coming first with ninety percent in my French exam in the first year. I also came first in Maths getting sixty eight percent in the third year. The teacher asked me to help my fellow pupils with the subject by going round to their desks when they put their hands up for help. Even doing that job I felt like a huge monster towering over them. The smallest job I had to do in public made me feel like the most self conscious person alive. Had I been getting a better private life and the encouragement I needed Daddy would have been proud to have owned such a daughter and that goes for all of his children. As for other subjects at school I hated PE or games as it was called. Worst of all was hockey as we had to play in the freezing cold. First we had a long walk to the fields opposite the school so were even colder by the time we started playing. Our legs got whacked with the stick more than the ball did. I was glad when we did not have to play that awful game anymore. When playing in the school fields I got a good spin on the discus but it never went very far. One afternoon I threw it and before I had time to see where it landed the sky became pitch dark; as though it was midnight but it was not an eclipse, as the following day in the newspaper there was a picture of one of the tallest buildings in the city where the top was seen as in broad daylight! It was only three o'clock.

'Leave everything exactly where it is!' shouted the teacher. 'Go back to the changing rooms and wait there.'

We changed quickly and went back to our classrooms. In that serious moment of awe the teacher led us in prayers and hymns to our Heavenly Father. She prepared us for the end of the world. It remained dark for three hours but we were not taken up to Heaven. Who wanted to face an angry God and even more punishment anyway? At least we had a good excuse for our late arrival home.

'What if, when I get home, my house has been struck by lightening and there's nothing but rubble?' I said to Penny, a small child with grey looking hair.

'Don't be so negative!' she sternly told me.

But little did she know why I said such a thing.

As for other sports activities swimming lessons were a flop. We went to the local swimming pool where the teacher instructed me,

'Go to the middle and swim back towards me.'

The swimming instructor stood beside her. While they chatted to each other I walked to within one foot of the edge, reached out with a crawl type arm gesture and grabbed the bar before I drowned! I was not being watched at all so never learned. I enjoyed cross-country running though. The freedom and space as I took over many of the other pupils gave me a sense of achievement. During the annual cross country run one year I lagged behind with the other girls but eventually came to my senses and left them to talk their miles away. As I sped over hill and dale I overtook what seemed like hundreds of people. If only I had thought to do that in the first place. I would have come in first or at least second. As it was, I came in forty eighth. The girls I left behind finished in the seventies position. Another day a girl named Alice who had become a friend naturally, as opposed to being asked to, did a sponsored walk with me around the field outside school. We walked round it eight times which equaled sixteen miles. We came in first and were proud to have achieved something of worth. Alice mentioned the Cheshire Evening Gazette had been there to take pictures. We were both disappointed in not being around for that but took it in our stride.

I had become extremely sad and negative with one blow after another and many times simultaneous blows coming from all directions. My confidence was dead and there was no hope of regaining it. Daddy never bought material for needlework classes. The teacher sent me instead to the cookery room to wash up for another class. Any common sense had been doused by my sense of inferiority. I knocked on the door of the classroom and embarrassingly entered. In front of the class, who were having a theory lesson, I asked the teacher if I could do any jobs for them. They would have known why I was sent. She pointed to the milk bottles standing at the sink,

'We need those bottles washing.'

There were about eight of them. So over and above the teacher's voice came that awful gurgling sound as I plunged one milk bottle after another into the water. There was no other way to wash them that I could think of. The teacher did not bother to reeducate me. Embarrassment is a mild word to use for the way I felt.

The only piece of material Daddy did give me was a pair of thick, black, herringbone curtains – I do not know what my teachers thought. One day I had a brain wave and went knocking on the doors in my neighbourhood asking people if they would like a dress making for any of their children. Most said no but there was one woman who opened the door and listened,

'Can I make a dress for your little girl for needlework at school? My dad won't buy me any material.' I showed her the pattern I had got from the needlework room. She was pleased with my offer. 'Please will you buy some material and let me have it. I think she'll look gorgeous in the dress I've chosen.'

She bought the material and a few days later off I went with the goods to school but I hated needlework because it was practical and having to move around the room made me feel really conspicuous. I had no idea what to do and was afraid to ask the teacher. By the end of term I still had not finished the dress and the child did without. I never wanted to see the mother again.

As time went on I began to get more agitated at my situation at home and looked again for a way to shorten the days. I scanned my mind for ideas and at last thought I found an answer. If telling and showing my teachers about the bruises did not work then surely the other problem would, so armed with that, I asked to see the headmistress. Once in her office I found I could not speak. She suggested,

'If you find it hard to say the words I can get you some paper and you can write it down.'

'Yes, okay, I'll do that.'

She got some paper from her desk and offered to leave the room while I wrote. In as much detail as I could I described my father's sexual abuse. Mrs Wayne read my account and promptly said,

'I'll deal with it.'

After a few days she sent for me,

'Somebody will come to your house and talk to your dad.'

'But that will only make things worse!'

Everything inside me froze.

My warning went unheeded. For the next few weeks every knock at the door was sure to bring instant trouble for us. Who would answer the door? I was upstairs when I heard the knock. Daddy answered it and I crept to the banister to determine who the caller was. I could not hear the caller's side of the conversation but could hear clearly some of what Daddy said,

'Rachel is handicapped,' and then more muffled words that I could not make out.

I guessed that was that. He closed the door after the short visit but did not come upstairs. His lie stunned me. Mrs Wayne never questioned me regarding a visit and no-one else called. My plan had failed.

Mrs Wayne was kind though and tried to help us when Peggy and I volunteered to help make egg mayonnaise sandwiches for a school event. We had not asked Daddy and knew he would be at home that Saturday. After the event Mrs Wayne wrapped up loads of left over sandwiches for us to take back and offered to give us a lift home. What a treat!

'Perhaps our dad won't get mad if I show him all the sandwiches,' I said fearfully.

Humouring him sometimes did the trick and it did that day.

Our idea of right and wrong was scrambled - everything we did or were doing was wrong even when we had done our best. Nothing we ever did of our own initiative was right especially when we heard from our house the rag and bone man shouting,

'Rag, bowne, rag bowne,'

He trotted along the road with his horse and cart. We searched the house looking for items to discard, thinking to please Daddy with what we got in exchange. Most of the rubbish was in the shed. I found a dirty old coat in there and ran out with it.

126

Samantha came out with me and together we chose a few dishes and plates in its place.

'Where did these bowls come from?' Daddy asked as soon as he saw them.

'The rag and bone man, we gave him a big, old coat from under the workbench.'

'That coat was a ground mat used for lying on while I'm under the car,' he told us but did not lose his temper; possibly because Mrs Fabican might turn up at any moment.

For many, growing up is an adventure but not for us and all children like to have pets. We were no exception. We had already tried to adopt a stray cat. We left him at home in the front room all day while we were at school. Our fireside rug was in an untidy state when we arrived home. When I opened it out I found he had covered up his mess. I was fascinated with his intelligence in doing so but it did nothing to allay my fears of Daddy's reactions. I shoved him out and that was that. Our second attempt at smuggling a pet home was when somebody from school told me she had some puppies and I said we would like to have one. She asked her mother if the puppy could come to us and her reply was,

'Mummy says you can only have him if your dad says so.'

'We'll ask him, okay,' knowing all the time that we could not have the dog.

Next day I assured the person Daddy said we could have the puppy so it was not long before I carried the tiny pup into our house. Peggy and Samantha's faces lit up. We had to get our heads together and plan how to keep him without Daddy ever knowing but William discovered we had him first and suggested getting a box.

'Okay, we'll get a box and keep him in it in our bedroom,' I decided.

Leaving the puppy in William's care we girls nipped round the shop for a big empty box. I put a small bit of old clothing in the bottom of it. Our own little black Labrador was placed in there. Daddy came in from work and, after his evening shave, wondered where a particular whimpering noise was coming from. I stood guard outside our bedroom. With shaving foam round his face and a razor in his hand he walked the couple of steps from the bathroom to our room. I could think of no way to restrain him.

'Let's have a look in here.'

He turned the knob and, fearing the worst, I held my breath. My father approached the box and saw the innocent looking puppy scampering around inside.

'Who gave you this?'

'A girl from school and we can't give her back, they won't take her.'

'Well, you can't have it here.'

The puppy had to go. Calling next door we asked the Barkson children if they wanted her. Nancy, there eldest who was Samantha's age, managed to get permission out of her mum to have it. Even though she was no longer ours we watched her grow. They called her Lassie, we had called her Sheba. A few months later I noticed Lassie had white powdery stuff around her nose and mouth. I thought she was too young to be going grey. Nancy informed me,

'It's distemper.'

Not long afterwards Lassie died and that was that.

So, there was no sign of entertainment for us but the yearly fair came to Blyster Park every Easter and one year Daddy allowed Richard, Peggy and Samantha to go but he said,

'Rachel, you go to Benediction with Alan.'

My heart sank and I lost my temper. Those displays of temper were never seen by Daddy but he was witness to that mild display as I was being separated from most of my siblings and from enjoying that one off chance of having a good time with them. I could not hold on any longer and stormed out of the front room. Grabbing the handle I pulled the door hard behind me which caught my foot. Terror flared as I walked upstairs. Daddy followed. He had been waiting for Mrs Fabican so perhaps that saved my skin. He raised his hand high to hit me and I shrunk away. Then he put his hand down but told me,

'You are not to go anywhere. Stay in your room.'

Then he went downstairs.

As I watched my brothers and sisters walk together across the green from the bedroom window Daddy went out with Mrs Fabican. Even though I had the house to myself I dared not leave the bedroom. What a time I had turning the recently cleaned room and neat pile of ironing into a blitzed warfare zone; hurling clothes, emptying drawers, yanking blankets and mattresses onto the floor. Shouts of anger erupted from a full heart. After my wrath was satisfied it was time to tidy up the mess and change the room round at the same time. My sympathy, though, was with Alan because he had gone to benediction alone. What do you do when your loyalties are so divided?

When my fourteenth birthday came around nothing was mentioned at all and, knowing it was never a time for a family celebration, I still decided to remind Daddy,

'It's my birthday tomorrow.'

He ignored me completely. I thought he had not heard so the next day I said again,

'It's my birthday today.'

He ignored me a second time. But Alan walked in that night with a present. I unwrapped it and to my amazement he had bought me an umbrella. At first I wondered if it really was for me but he assured me it was. My very own blue umbrella, it had to rain plenty after that.

Not long after that Alan moved out. Daddy more than likely insisted on it as there was not enough room for all seven of us living in that house. Alan had been sleeping on the pulled down settee. The same settee I had slept in with Nanny all those years ago. Richard left home to live with Alan on his eighteenth birthday carrying a brown paper bag with his meager possessions inside. His only clothes were what he stood up in. He was so fed up with Daddy taking all the money he earned and the whole regime of Mrs Fabican's presence, though not with us, which he felt counted for the way we were all treated by Daddy.

Our home was a prison. We were not allowed to go to the cinema, fetes, fairs, swimming, school sports days or any other event without our father's express permission. Our lives were practically null and void. As I had never been to a school sports day and my years at school were nearing an end, I desperately wanted to go to it that year. After asking my father if we could go he said no but William took it upon himself to allow both Peggy and I to go, saying,

'It's okay, you go to it and I'll tell Dad I punished you when you got home.'

So both Peggy and I went along. The sun shone for the whole of that summer evening but a dark cloud of instability hovered over us and underneath, uncertainty and fear took firm hold of every step we took. When we arrived home later William said he had had to tell Dad where we were but,

'Tell you what. Get ready for bed then kneel down on the floor in your pyjamas. Dad said you have to be up when he gets in.' so we kneeled but not on the carpet because it did not stretch to the walls. 'Just kneel for an hour and I'll tell Dad you've been there for three, then he probably won't hit you.'

The cold, dark brown, stone floor did not get any softer or warmer as we knelt; neither did our knee caps which only became number until we could no longer feel them! Only a dread of what might happen pervaded the atmosphere. Around midnight we heard the back door knob turn. Our hearts leapt in shock. Daddy opened the second door and entered our company. Immediately, William told him,

'They've had their punishment.'

He was satisfied with that and we went to bed unscathed.

We often prayed to God for help but He never showed up. Being practical I decided to put Him out of the front room one day. *Perhaps the devil will help?* I encouraged my sisters,

'Let's empty the front room of the holy pictures and things to do with God.'

We put them out in the hall then cut paper into twenty six squares and wrote out the letters of the alphabet one by one on each. I brought a glass from the kitchen into the front room. I had heard about this while I was living at Lincrest.

'Right, we'll sit round and see if it works.'

'Is anybody there?' I spelt out with the glass.

Putting my hand lightly over it we waited for an answer. Nothing happened at all. No-one, not God, nor the devil wanted anything to do with us. We were left to ourselves with still no way out. Even so, every Sunday we went to Mass. Daddy did not come with us, ever. He went to St Mary's in Upper Hockbury. Often he wanted to know what the sermon was about; just to be sure we went. He need not have bothered because we always dutifully attended.

Sometimes at weekends Daddy showed us some of his Royal Navy exercises. The star jump,

'You do it like this.'

He squatted down on his haunches and, while jumping, shot his hands and legs out as though towards outer corners of a rectangle. The most fascinating exercise was when he put two chairs at a distance with the seats facing each other and taught Alan how to levitate,

'Lie down with your feet on one chair and your head on the other. There has to be nothing in the middle.'

Alan managed to balance perfectly with his arms by his sides. After that Daddy hypnotized me, during which he said,

'You will not wake up until I click my fingers.' I was aware of everything throughout the procedure. I did not lose consciousness or go into a dream state. He continued, 'You can go now.'

I walked about for a while then returned to tell him,

'I still feel funny when I'm walking around.'

He clicked his fingers and instantly I was free. He only demonstrated that performance once.

An inexplicable occurrence happened one Saturday morning after that day. On waking I felt that my body was about to break. My arms were straight down by my sides and I lay confused in the bed.

'How did I get like this?' I asked my sisters who took no notice.

They carried on playing in the bedroom, not realizing my condition. The top sheet clung to my rigid arms. I could not even wiggle a finger. The bound sheet created a heavy crushing sensation right across my chest. At least I could breathe. Not saying another word a feeling of deep isolation penetrated the room. I was on my own in the problem. My sisters were deaf to my calling. My fourteen year old body lay paralyzed by the sheet while my mind tried to solve the problem. I gazed, with lifted head, at the tightly twisted sheet which had been firmly and neatly tucked under the mattress, either side of my feet. I was wrapped like a mummy. *How can I get out?* The answer came eventually. *I'll have to twist.* With all my strength I tried to move. The near impossible attempts finally made way for me to roll over. After the first roll the sheet was just as tight, and the next, and the next. It took twenty one twists to get out. It still remains a mystery as to how I got like that in the first place. Why had I not woken up when I was being so meticulously wrapped around and around? And who on earth was responsible? Had I done it myself in my sleep? I hardly think so.

A few months after that and still only fourteen, my father arranged a job interview for me. He explained,

'You will live in a family as a mother's help.'

He drove me to a Jewish home quite a few miles away. The family seemed nice enough people. The lady of the house spoke pleasantly and I wanted her to accept me. Her hair, unusually dark, matched her tanned complexion. I would have done anything to take her aside and beg her to let me live there.

'I can see you would work well here,' she said, 'but you are too young. If you were fifteen we would employ you.'

I stood pleading with my eyes but she was oblivious to my cry and while travelling home with Daddy I wondered again how much longer I would have to live with him. Such was my frustration at times that I sat on my bed; the bottom bunk, and hit the top of my head hard against the green, iron ridge jutting down from the top bunk. Pain seared through my unsuspecting body. Many times I punched myself on the side of the head with both fists as hard as I possibly could and pulled my hair. I did not know that I had become mentally and emotionally disturbed.

Chapter Six

Leaving Home and Reporting my Father

I had not finished my fourth year at school when Daddy forced me to leave. It was the Easter term and I was fifteen and a half. He took me to an agency in Siverton, Lancashire, who found another vacancy for a mother's help. The house in Rasworth, also in Lancashire, was where my second interview took place with Mr and Mrs Shabbery. Thankfully, I was accepted. A well kept garden greeted us as we drove up the hilly drive. Mrs Shabbery was impressed with me and my father put on his wonderful middle class image. I think if Mrs Shabbery had taken me aside and talked to me in private I would have told her all about myself, holding nothing back, but she was oblivious to my dilemma. One actor and one little actress played their parts well. We left the beautiful big house to go home and collect my belongings. On my second arrival I was shown to my bedroom and left to unpack. I was frightened but soon got to know the routine of the house and what was expected of me.

The Shabbery's twins, Paulette and Paula, were five years old and their son Matthew, thirteen. He was on holiday from boarding school and due to return after the Easter holidays. I had become so scared that I found it hard to speak to them. Mrs Shabbery did not have a name as far as I was concerned. I felt self conscious if I even dreamed of calling her. If I wanted her I had to look directly into her face or else she would not know who I was speaking to.

I learned a few ways of proper living there, though not many and, as I had done to my sisters, told the girls horror stories. My intention was to prepare them for the nastier things in life that they were sure to face. They did not seem to be aware of any so I made sure they would know how to escape when the inevitable encounter arose.

In time I came to love Mrs Shabbery more as a mother than an employer and became confronted for the first time away from home with my deepest longing but could not express it. It would not have been right as an employee anyway.

During the summer holidays we all went to Boster Bay in Wales for a month. I mixed up the holiday with work and on one occasion refused to look after the girls. Matthew was also with us and I had a few boating lessons from him. He tried desperately to help me keep the boat on the water but it was no use. I steered onto the rocks, maybe just because they were there. Going the wrong way was certainly nothing new to me.

Matthew, being only two years younger than me, did not need any looking after but the girls needed constant supervision. Paula was an easy child to care for but Paulette, rather bad tempered and difficult. They were both lovely but who needed two Paulettes? Certainly not Mrs Shabbery.

The view from the bungalow lounge windows portrayed storms as majestic paintings. Early one morning a bagpiper's tunes were carried across the grey sea by the boisterous wind, and faraway rocks added the necessary height for us to be able to see him. I wondered what bagpipes were doing in Wales.

One day we went to see some friends of the Shabbery's and, not knowing how to behave, I sat on a chair at the far side of the room for the duration of the visit. The fear was so great I was unable to move, even to go to the toilet. Three hours later it was time to go and the friends discovered there had been someone else in the room, however, not until I prized myself from the chair.

My hunger for a mother grew in intensity and that void needed to be filled if I was to make any progress in my growing up stage. I had been starved of affection for the whole of my lifetime. Perhaps being in the presence of a loving family caused the hunger to rise to the surface and it became difficult to deal with as time went by. One night I refused to go to bed after Mrs Shabbery showed me the insides of a freshly caught fish. The closeness of that encounter made me feel somewhat like a daughter and I did not want it to end. The insides of the fish were still moving; just like mine. My stomach churned every second of every day and her presence comforted me a little. As I watched the fish being prepared for cooking I planned my next move which was to stay up all night due to the grief of not being a real daughter. How could I voice what was going on? When she finished I sat at a table, silently refusing to budge while she tried to say goodnight. I ignored her as I sat with my throat constricted with the pain. She was at her wits end when an hour later I still had not moved. The evening was disastrous and ended with Mrs Shabbery shouting,

'You're just as bad as Paulette!'

The comment sliced into me. I felt thoroughly rejected and what I was hoping to achieve did not come to pass. She at last went to bed and I was left alone. I was going the wrong way in trying to find the love I craved but what other way could I have gone? That night I slept in my day clothes. What if I had gone up to Mrs Shabbery and sat on her lap or cuddled up to her? That, I am sure, would have had the same result. It did not even occur to me to do that. I simply acted like a five year old turning sixteen. And so we left the Bay with bitter memories, at least concerning me.

I had thought that once I left home everything would be fine but that was not the case. My distorted personality had not been left behind. The absence of my mother and the stamp of my father had pressed too deeply into my soul, leaving their indelible wounds. At times I wondered where we would be and what we would be like if our mother had not died. Would we be in Australia? Would we be geniuses? I know we would all have been a great asset to society.

I was frightened to do anything out of the ordinary. When I did I made terrible blunders and after attempting anything outside of my normal behaviour I sprung back into my shell, abhorring my own presence. About a week after the holiday Mrs Shabbery introduced me to another mother's help named Diane who lived down the road. Diane's family had a kitten. Mine had a little French bulldog called Dumpling. I took the little brown dog round to Diane's a few days after we were acquainted. The children were with her in the garden as she held their kitten in her arms. Its sweet looks caused Dumpling's head to move from side to side. As he whined I thought to myself, *Dumpling loves the kitten; let him loose to have a closer look.* I sympathetically let him off the lead but before I stood up he pounced on the kitten ferociously; barking and biting, scratching and clawing the little body until the blood ran freely and the kitten almost torn in two. The poor thing nearly died. I tried to get Dumpling to stop but had no power to tackle him. He slipped through my fingers like running water as I tried to get hold of him. I never knew Dumpling to be that way, ever. Normally he was so much fun. He was not so sweet after all and I would never give him the benefit of the doubt again. A dog is a dog and it cannot think the same way as humans do regarding cats. Dogs are their enemies but you do see them as companions sometimes. I think that is only when they have grown up together. I did have fun teasing him when we were alone in the house. Several times a day while everybody was out I went outside, rang the doorbell, dashed into the lounge and hid behind the door. He scampered to the front door hoping to find a visitor. I jumped out of hiding and made a great fuss of him. It greatly entertained us both. Being a carefree person in front of people was impossible and only led to guilt and a blushing onslaught.

Thursdays were my days off and most times I visited home, carefully avoiding 'Daddy' times. When he was in, however, I gave him money and chocolates.

One day while I was in Rasworth I heard that Samantha had been admitted to Toy Town hospital to have her appendix taken out so I took it upon myself to visit her. It was not hard to find her bed as it was just to the left of the entrance to the ward. We chatted and laughed but laughing for her was not a joyful occasion. She told me very seriously,

'Don't make me laugh cos it hurts, and it hurts when I bend.'

I hated any of my family suffering. I could not understand why they had to at all. But then, that is what a mother is there for; to care. I had done my best from the age of six. Samantha was a brave 'daughter' at twelve and only three years younger than me. Of course, I always knew Peggy and Samantha were my sisters but I had a responsibility to fulfill as well. I was afraid of being on the ward in case Daddy visited her unexpectedly. Trembling, I asked,

'When are you coming out?'

'On Thursday.'

'Is anybody coming to get you and take you home?'

'No.'

Anger surfaced. I stared into outer space for a moment and then said with determination and finality,

'Well, I'll come and get you then.'

I felt ten inches taller. Thankfully, she still had her clothes in her locker so collecting them from home would not be a problem. As it was my day off it would also not be a problem for the Shabbery's to let me go. When I arrived to take her home Samantha got dressed slowly and we walked the whole length of the cinder path. For her to walk all that way was a very painful exercise.

As my sisters were not taken care of I planned to take Samantha for a visit to Rasworth without asking Daddy. Peggy wanted to come as well and followed us all the way to Dillthorpe Railway Station where a lot of reasoning went on between her begging to come and my determination to avoid trouble for either of them with Daddy. I was afraid for both her and Samantha. The dilemma was, should I say yes and cause Daddy to batter them both or should I send her home? There was no way of knowing what he would do but one thing I was certain of; he would be mad either way. I reasoned Peggy's presence at home would placate him somewhat. I can still see her standing, looking disappointed and longing to come. I would have had no trouble letting her if Daddy was not an issue. I also had to think about the Shabbery's and how they would cope with two of my sisters coming for the day. I had not asked them. Daddy did not like being shown up in front of people. I knew that if he knew Mr Shabbery thought he was a bad man there would be even more trouble. Another thing to consider was that if he had known Samantha and Peggy had had a nice day and had a happy time with me he would have wiped more than the floor with them. I had no choice but to say no and send her home. If that was today, being older and wiser, I would have done differently but at fifteen it was far from easy to choose what was the very best. I told her,

'Don't say anything to Daddy when he asks you where Samantha is.'

In her loyalty she did not but he adamantly questioned her about where Samantha was. She told me later that he punched her hard in the face, my little thirteen year old sister. She ran upstairs with a nose bleed then he showed a little humanity by putting a cold flannel on her forehead. She froze at his touch. If I regretted anything it is that decision. Even up to this day I have not been able to forgive myself. I am pretty sure she has not either. Unless she tells me she understands and forgives me it will remain that way forever. She has chosen over time to have nothing to do with me and has not spoken to me for ten long years. I long for her return and think of her daily. I pray that one day she will lift the burden from my shoulders. I cannot lift it off myself. I cannot tell myself she forgives me and put words into her mouth. Come back, Peggy, let us be friends again.

Samantha and I told the Shabbery's about Daddy and that we feared for Peggy. I feared for Samantha going back to face him and she feared for herself. If two of them came it would have been far worse for both of them. Mr Shabbery offered,

'I'll tell you what, I'll take you home and tell your dad you've had a good day.'

It was not a good thing to say to my father. He never wanted us happy. After a long drive and telling him all about the problems at home we walked Samantha to the front door. My father opened it to our knock. I wondered how Peggy was doing and wanted to see her but could not, we were not invited in. After Samantha went in she exchanged a pleasant plastic smile to Mr Shabbery, who said to Daddy,

'She's had a lovely time.'

My father thanked him profusely for looking after Samantha. I could only imagine what went on once the door was closed.

Underneath the trauma, our love, albeit confused and torn, was firm and nobody was going to take that away, at least not from me. Under the circumstances our relationships were put under tremendous strain. We never had a good time together without looking over our shoulders for the ton of guilt about to blast any fun out of existence. Samantha, I knew, would suffer for her day out with me. It disturbed me a lot that my sisters were at home without me to protect them. The only way I could do that was to try to avoid trouble in the first place. There was no way I could stand up to my father, no way any of us could. What if Daddy did to them what he had been doing to me – sexually? I thought it my duty to get them out if I could. The day after Samantha came to the Shabbery's I told Mrs Shabbery about Daddy carrying me into his bed at midnight. She suggested I go to the NSPCC, so on my next day off I went to see them in Centon. I was wondering where to go once inside the building when a man walked past me along a corridor. I followed slightly behind as he was in a hurry and asked,

'Who do I see if I want to report something my Dad does to me?'

'What does he do?'

'Makes me get into bed with him.'

'Oh, go to the police,' he said in a cold, calculating way.

First though, I needed to obtain my sisters' permission and paid a visit home. It was difficult as I did not know if they would turn against me for thinking such a thing. Samantha was standing by the kitchen sink when I asked,

'Do you mind if I go to the police about Daddy?'

I was not ready for her reply after I divulged all he had done to me.

'Oh, he's been doing that to us, too! And when you come home to visit he says, "I sent her away to get rid of her but she keeps coming back."'

'Does he? Did he?' I asked bewildered.

I did not know what I had done that was so bad to be continually hated by him. Did the money and chocolates not tell him I forgave him and that I was good?

'But how can he have been doing that to you? He was always doing it to me!'

'When we took the tea up answering his knocks…'

'Ah.'

Then I understood why neither of them wanted to go upstairs at those times. My intentions to save them were too late. The abuse had to be stopped there and then! An hour later I was on my way to fulfill a mission I had always wanted to each time we ran away; to rescue my family. When I arrived at the police station at five o'clock it was already dark and I was taken to a large room where two policemen and two policewomen questioned me intensely all at once. The policemen sat opposite me and the women sat to my left. I sat with the window on my right. Nobody was beside me. I was told to write out a statement. A police officer handed me the required paperwork but I could not even start.

'Do you mean I should write all the words exactly as it happened? I have to write the words?'

'Yes.'

'I have to tell you about what he did to me exactly as it happened, like what he did to me while in his bed? I have to say it all the way it happened?'

'Yes.'

'Alright,' I took a deep breath. The pencil stayed in my hand. I held it tight while trying to think of the words to say, 'you mean I have to say bra and things?'

'Yes.'

And on it went. The policewomen took over the session and because I had so much difficulty writing the words and describing exactly what my father had done in detail, it took them three hours to put together a reasonable statement. They had taken the paper off me and written it themselves as I could not put one word on paper. As I sat in anguish I longed for my mother to drop out of Heaven. The familiar lump grew in my throat till it felt like the size of a football. I found it increasingly hard to swallow and knew that I could not hold on for much longer. A couple of minutes later I broke down in an avalanche of heart breaking sobs,

'So you're making it all up now, are you?' one policewoman asked.

What? I sat in disbelief that they even considered such a thing. They were not my friends after all. Why had I bothered? I felt like a criminal and stared through the window at the dark outside. Some of the police men and women moved from the table while others watched over me in silence. It was over, my father was reported. What were they going to do? One of the policemen came back into the room, stood by the table and explained,

'A detective has gone to your house to arrest your father and will bring your sisters in for questioning.'

I thought they had not believed me! Then I suddenly froze and begged,

'No, don't bring him in here.'

'You will not see your father,' they assured me but as I looked out of the window in trepidation every face I saw was Daddy's. What fear! What utter dread, even feeling unprotected in the police station!

In the meantime the events at my family's house were as usual except that Mrs Fabican had come over. That was a rare, if ever, thing for her to do at that time in the evening. Was God at work? Samantha had gone to bed and Daddy was upstairs getting ready to go out. There was a knock at the door. I had warned Peggy,

'Someone might come to the door. If they do, say you don't know anything about it,' to avoid her getting into trouble or beaten up.

When the foreboding knock rattled the house Peggy opened it to a policeman, a policewoman and possibly a social worker or plain clothed detective. The uniformed policeman greeted her,

'Hello, Peggy, is your dad in?'

She did not know how he knew it was her, perhaps I had described her. Peggy was immediately in a fluster and ran upstairs as fast as possible. She blurted out almost incoherently,

'Daddy, Daddy, da, da, da, Daddy, Daddy, the police are at the door and I don't know anything about it, I don't know anything about it, I don't know anything about it,' Daddy turned round and in a flat tone said,

'William!'

But little did he know William was not the one they were after. However, it had a tremendous calming effect on Peggy. The threat was off. Peggy went back to tell the police he would be down but he was right behind her. Daddy commanded,

'Go upstairs.'

He invited the police into the front room. I will never know the conversation that went on in there but a little later Mrs Fabican went upstairs to Peggy and Samantha,

'Samantha, get dressed and Peggy don't get ready for bed. The police are taking you to the station.'

At that moment Daddy went upstairs and said,

'Come on, we're going.'

In the car Daddy was excusing himself profusely saying, 'Rachel's always telling stories.'

Well, that was true, I was always telling Peggy and Samantha detective and other stories in the night before we went to sleep but how was he to know? That is, when I was allowed to go to my own bed. I told them about the notorious yeti who lived in Blyster Park, 'He comes round at midnight. He is as tall as the houses and can see in through the bedroom windows. He will be able to see if you are asleep. He's coming in a minute. It's nearly twelve o'clock. I can see his shadow.' I frightened both them and myself so much that we all hid under our covers hoping not to be seen.

At the police station my sisters were brought to the room next to mine. Samantha told them her experiences as they wrote them down for her. Peggy's descriptions of the details entertained the police women so much that they, 'preferred that real life drama to the cinema'.

After questioning we were taken somewhere to be physically examined. Peggy was extremely upset by the events and I was not too keen either. They wanted to take my mortified sister in first but she requested,

'Let Rachel go first then I will.'

Her plea was ignored. They found no evidence to convict our father in any of us because he had known how far to go without being detected. He himself had checked me one day when he told me to get in the bath. He came in fully dressed and told me to stand before him while he felt around inside with his finger and it really hurt but he only did that once. There was no explanation given, just the cold act then he left.

When the harrowing evening came to an end at approximately eleven o'clock Peggy and Samantha were taken into care; Samantha for the very first time. I did not see them leave. I went back to Rasworth.

My sisters were kept together, spending the first night at Gilder House, a children's home in Pomiston, where they were promptly beaten up, as if they had not had enough. Then they were taken to a Salvation Army children's home in Bealshaw for about two months and after that were back in Cheshire with a Catholic Charity.

The phone rang a week or so later, Mrs Shabbery answered then handed it to me. I was summonsed to a magistrate's court by one of the detectives on our case. A few days later the three of us girls stood in front of Daddy in the small court room. The magistrate never spoke to us, only to him. His answers to the magistrate's questions were mostly,

'Yes, me-Lud' or 'No, me-Lud'

Me-Lud? What's a Lud? It sounded ridiculous to me and all at once he was like a little boy, having been disarmed from all power against us but he pleaded not guilty. I felt thoroughly dissatisfied with that but it did not end there. In the following weeks and months we were backwards and forwards to court but each time were sent home as Daddy's constant plea remained, 'not guilty'. One more phone call from the detective in charge came to the house. Mrs Shabbery answered. The detective on the case told her what I was to expect and she passed it on to me,

'Your father has said he wants to stand trial.' What did I know about trial? Mrs Shabbery went on to explain, 'He is trying to frighten you into withdrawing your accusations.'

'Why should I withdraw anything? It's all true.'

I did not understand.

The day came for our attendance at the Crown Court in Cheshire where we sat on a bench outside the courtroom waiting for our turn to be heard. The nuns from Pomiston came to support us. I could not see Daddy as he was sitting on our side near the front doors of the courtroom and a few people sat beside him blocking the view, I had not noticed if they were anybody we knew. We waited for a long time and then a man approached both me and my sisters. *Is this it? Are we going in?*

'Your dad's pleaded guilty.' He announced.

So it was all off again. My chance for emotional freedom had been stripped away and I felt empty and hopeless. I wanted to tell the 'world' about my suffering, to be properly rescued and to be helped and comforted. I wanted my sisters to be comforted and to leave it all behind in the courtroom. In a strange way though, I was slightly relieved at the plea. He had told the truth! We went back to our various homes.

I found out later that he was given two years probation. The news was most unwelcome because I knew if he and I were walking around the streets of Cheshire at any given time I could bump into him and that was terrifying. Acute fear claimed me as its victim and it was I who was imprisoned, not him. If the violence had been missing from his character it would have been easier to cope with. I was already suffering with excruciating pains in my temples which only eased by pressing hard against them with my fingers. I was a very frightened, distressed young girl. Eventually, I went to see the doctor and told him my life story. He listened without interrupting and then exclaimed,

'I don't know how you've done it.'

I had taken it all in my stride but what I did not know was that the strength I displayed had undetectably destroyed and eaten me away on the inside.

Whilst at the Shabbery's I bought a bicycle from one of Mr Shabbery's stores in Sunbarton. He was the manager and owned the stores. Often, I cycled many miles to visit my sisters. A feeling of deep isolation was creeping over me. Peggy lived at Greentree House, Pomiston, for the older girls and Samantha at Wallflower House, also in Pomiston. On one of those visits the three of us planned a day to go to our house in Hockbury to pick up some of our belongings; not when Daddy would be in but William. He had to be in or it would have been a wasted journey. We went round the back of the maisonettes to see if Daddy's car was there. It was not, so we walked back round to the front door and knocked. William answered,

'What do you want?' he was oblivious as to what had gone on.

'We've come to get our things, let us in to get them.'

We tore upstairs and scrambled to collect everything we could from the bedroom and left as soon as possible. We had to leave our wooden boxes that Uncle Len made behind, as we had no room to take them. There was one special item missing. Sister Agatha had given me a holy water font in the shape of a little altar boy while I was at Lincrest. Daddy must have taken it down and thrown it away. I treasured it.

'Where's my altar boy? It was hanging on the wall there.'

I pointed to the nail he had hung from, opposite the front door.

'I don't know.' William answered, unmoved by our sudden appearance.

'Now it's gone.'

I looked here and there and it had not been placed in our bedroom. I had not only lost my mother and father but assumed my brothers knew about the reporting and did not believe Daddy treated us that way and had turned against us. We took our things and left.

Back at the Shabbery's, a few weeks later, the telephone rang. Mrs Shabbery was out so I answered it. On the other end a female voice told me,

'I saw the advertisement in the paper for a mother's help.'

'They've got a mother's help,' I informed her and put the phone down.

When I mentioned it to Mrs Shabbery on her return she was angry and said,

'You should have told her I was not in and to phone back later.'

She then very politely told me I would have to go and arranged for a Child Care Officer to organize something else. It came as a real shock. I thought she cared. She used to laugh at my outbursts of anger when the bacon would not cook properly or the toast burnt; just to cheer me up I suppose. I felt reasonably safe there. Maybe it was all the club biscuits that went missing from the store cupboard. They, in their red wrappers, once carefully removed, were irresistible and as there were so many in the box, how would she even notice them gone?

She explained about the story telling. How it disturbed her girls. I had never known it disturbed them and felt betrayed. Why was I not told before? However, I could not argue. Dumbfounded, I prepared for my next journey into oblivion.

Chapter Seven

Cadet Nurse in a Private Hospital

Miss Callipart, the Child Care Officer, found a foster home in Blackhurst, Lancashire and introduced me to the Pockburn family. There were other foster children but Annabelle, a nine year old, was Mrs Pockburn's own daughter. Mrs Pockburn did not have a husband. The house was an ordinary family home, not at all elaborate in comparison to Rasworth.

On my second day I sat and knitted, trying to keep myself to myself and despite giving people the cold shoulder, people insisted on talking to me. I hated it. I had, after all, been double crossed by somebody I looked up to and admired. I did not like it there and wondered how long I would have to stay.

My bed had a thick, hard, yellow, plastic covering on the mattress which dipped a great hollow in the middle and was most uncomfortable. I had to get away! So my escape was planned. The following day after breakfast when everybody left the house I waited a quarter of an hour to make sure they were well gone. On the way out of the front door I left it on the catch in case Mrs Pockburn could not get in but pulled it tightly shut ensuring it would not swing open of its own accord.

Wearing the new white shoes I bought in Rasworth before I left I set off to walk the seven miles to Sunbarton. Once on the main road I followed the signposts and it was not long before blisters and sores taunted me along the route. The irritating stickiness held me up quite a bit until, at last, I reached Sunbarton and from there found my way back to the Shabbery's quite easily. Mrs Shabbery did not entertain my plea for clemency. She contacted the Social Services. Miss Callipart arrived soon afterwards to take me back to Blackhurst. I told them I was not happy and did not want to stay. My father's programming of getting a hiding purred away and sure enough when we arrived there was Mrs

Pockburn with chubby hands to plump hips. As soon as we entered the house she demanded,

'I think we deserve an apology, don't we?'

I apologised but neither she nor Miss Callipart seemed bothered about why I had run. Once Miss Callipart left, Mrs Pockburn took me on a tour round the house pointing at the walls where Annabelle had written, 'I love Rachel'. The statement sounded like the sickest thing I had ever heard and I did not yield to the guilt feelings I sensed were expected of me. How could she love me when I had only just arrived? Nothing changed my mind. Love was empty words. A lot would be expected of me if I stayed, after all I was the eldest in the household and most of the responsibility would fall on me and I was tired of life already.

A few days later Miss Callipart contacted me again with the suggestion that I work at a private hospital as a cadet nurse. It was run by nuns and I could live in. I did not like the sound of it but after the experience with the Pockburn's of, by then, only two weeks, I would go anywhere.

'Think about it,' said Miss Callipart.

It was a leap in the dark. I had nothing to lose. If I gained nothing what did it matter? Anyway, I was used to nuns. Almost immediately I phoned her back to accept. She collected me the next day and took me to St Chad's Hospital, Cheshire. Not long after I arrived I met Sister Kevin who was in charge of Swanfold; the mansion of a nurse's home consisting of four floors. I was shown my bed in room seven on the first floor where I left my sparse belongings before being taken downstairs. All the bedrooms were divided by pale green wooden partitions. Some slept two, some three and some four cadets to a room. The girls were being punished for some reason so were not down the 'cellar' when I was introduced to it. It was located in the basement and was the leisure area with a reading room, a lounge and a television room. I was stunned by the old bus seats that lined the walls in all three rooms but kept my feelings to myself. Most of the girls came over from Ireland to work.

The following day I was fitted with a cadet nurses uniform which consisted of a dark blue, below the knee, short sleeved dress; five clean, crisp aprons, a starched flat cap and a half length red cape. We had to fold the caps into shape and keep them in place with hair grips.

For the first week or two I worked on Chestnut Ward *(which catered for twelve patients, each with a room of their own, six on each side)* in knee socks because wearing tights signified adulthood which I refused to enter. Sister Benedict, who was in charge of the main office insisted, when she could not stand the sight any longer,

'Helen, please take Rachel to the shop and buy her some tights.'

Helen was a cadet who had been there for a year already and a stranger to me. With those tights on I screamed silently for a long time. The new image did not feel right at all. I soon got to know the routine and different patients requirements. They were elderly and some quite ill and dying. Sister Henry who was in charge was tall, quite stocky in build and a strict dragon. I was terrified of her. A smile never crossed her enormous face. One day she caught me carrying an empty commode pan against my apron and, instead of explaining what I was doing wrong, gave me a telling off I would never forget.

I could not mix with any of the girls and spent most of my off duty and evenings leaning against the hot radiator in Swanfold outside the office, opposite the kitchen. When I finally found the nerve to go into the kitchen one evening I started a habit of drinking a glass of milk and crunching the ice cubes I had added. None of the nuns agreed it was good for my teeth but I knew my teeth could chew through rocks and come to no harm. Not that I had tried. After quite a long stint on Chestnut Ward I was transferred to the geriatric open ward; the only open ward, apart from the children's ward, in the hospital. I was not impressed with the experience of stripping urine ridden, ammonia smelling and often soiled draw sheets from the elderly patients' beds and sluicing them in a huge sink in a room at the side of the ward. After two weeks I was thankfully moved on. Besides, the open ward made me feel conspicuous in full view of all and sundry. I preferred to work in more confined places.

The next ward was Sycamore Ward which was located on the main ground floor where 'normal' patients were cared for. That was far better, I felt, as it gave me a sense of importance and that I was doing something more worthwhile. It had a proper hospital atmosphere with doctors in white coats with stethoscopes hanging round their necks, or swinging from their hands, while visiting patients in their private rooms. I learned to take patients blood pressures and temperatures. During the week theatre trolleys were rolled to and fro along the corridors, up the lift and along the corridor adjacent to Chestnut Ward to the theatre where the patients were operated on. I often took them to the anaesthetic room and collected them from the recovery room after their operations. The cadet nurses also served meals on trays to the patients. I learned how to carry a full tray on one hand swiftly and effortlessly, fully confident it was quite safe and well balanced. The other hand being free to knock on and open doors and drag bed tables to the patient's bedsides where delighted people said thank you with a broad smile. Afternoons were fairly quiet and our evenings, after duty, were spent in Swanfold. Some of us went every evening into the chapel for Mass. The balcony of the chapel was at the further end of Chestnut Ward where we could look down on the chapel proper.

After a few weeks on Sycamore Ward I was moved yet again, for reasons unbeknown to me, to help out on the ward that cared for the elderly nuns in their private rooms – Alder Ward. I thought I would be better working on my own there but was eventually moved to the least of the wards; Elm, which had only five rooms and a kitchen at the top of a spiral staircase. It felt spooky and isolated, being cut off from the rest of the hospital, as if it did not belong there at all. Sally, a girl who had been at the hospital longer than me and who had become a friend, shared responsibility with me for it but we worked on different days. She was a wild girl and so perhaps that is why she was placed separately from the others, like I had been. But it was not long before they moved me again, after a very short time on Elm, back to Alder Ward where I stayed until I left the hospital. The elderly nuns were quite easy to care for as most were independent. I loved taking some who required it to chapel in their wheelchairs. After helping them in and making sure they were securely sitting with their feet on the footrests, I released the break, grabbed the handles and sped, one nun a time, along the ground floor of the hospital *(Sycamore Ward)* to the front row of the chapel. With each separate trip I tried to break the speed record; never once thinking of the poor nuns going ahead of me and what they were experiencing. I loved it and became mesmerized in my new found hobby. When Mass was over I raced at equal speed to collect them and returned them to their rooms. Once there I helped them out of their wheelchairs and sat them back in their armchairs like clockwork. I did not have one complaint neither did I fear one.

It was Sister Bernard's turn one afternoon and as usual the dust flew off the green lino as we passed the main entrance, the office, the patient's bedroom doors on right and left, sharp turned right and passed the main kitchen, more patient's doors on right and left and finally the entrance to the cadet nurse's canteen where I stopped just beyond it, stepped in front of Sister Bernard, opened the door of the chapel and led her quickly to the front of the pews, turned her chair in a three point turn and left her there. It was a peaceful and quiet Sunday. After Mass, I collected her and sped back the way I came along Sycamore Ward and up the Alder Ward corridor. A door opened just ahead of me to the right but it was too late. The wheelchair would not slow down and a tall, lanky Sister Richard strode forth without looking. Her shin took the full force of the impact. As my natural reaction to accidents was to laugh that was all I could do *(apologetically)* while Sister Richard hopped about for relief of pain.

For the nuns' dinners I had to go up to the convent kitchen. Once there, I stood like a statue. Fear was ever present when I saw Sister Michael, who cooked the meals. She was small but quite a moody nun. I found it difficult to ask for the meals and it was there that I developed a persecution complex; Sister Lucy, who worked in the sewing room, was getting something from the kitchen at the same time as me one day and started to sing,

'Where's yer mama gone, where's yer mama gone?'

She sang it all the time I was in there. I felt the cruelty of the song penetrate me and could not wait to get away. Finally, after collecting the meals for the nuns, I fled the kitchen as fast as I could to feed my hungry patients.

Mostly on Alder Ward my life was one big trance. I entertained myself while cleaning sinks and baths, constantly daydreaming of having parents and what my life would have been like if my mother had never died. Those daydreams inspired me to write poems about my experiences and it became a pastime for both me and Peggy.

While off duty at Swanfold we young nurses were taken care of mainly by Sister Kevin. She and I were always at loggerheads. Different girls gravitated towards different nuns, rather as mother figures and the girls therefore were known as that particular sister's pet or favourite. Sister Kevin sometimes inspected our rooms and searched the cupboards, until she came to mine, that is. My arms pressed against the partitions blocking her entry. I never had anything to hide but resented the intrusion and always won but, I might add, after a lengthy battle of wills.

Three nuns lived in Swanfold. Every night the sister on duty carried out a ten o'clock round, saying goodnight and turning the lights out. They changed what rooms we were in a few times. Most of us wanted room two which had only two beds but we were not granted it. That room was always occupied by Sadie and Evelyn who were close friends from Ireland and Sister Kevin's pets.

A new nun by the name of Sister Emmanuel came to Swanfold about six months after me. She was Vietnamese like Sister Kevin, was a very hard worker, great sport and a good laugh. It was a breath of fresh air when she arrived and we all got on with her very well. She was on our level with no barriers up; no air of superiority.

As for the girls I would do anything for them, after eventually getting used to them, except buy cigarettes. If they needed elastic bands for their hair, hair grips or apron strings, Rachel would supply. I kept a stock of most things and the girls knew where to come. As well as my angelic nature, there was the mischievous side so a few practical jokes were not amiss. I heard of the bucket on top of the door antic and decided Sister Emmanuel would be the best sport to do it on so one night before the round I told the girls what I intended to do. They were not so eager. However, once I made my mind up there was no going back. The bin, full of rubbish, perched on top of the slightly open door. We all waited in bed for the great moment. Sister was next door saying goodnight and it was our turn next. In she walked but not a sound was heard. Not understanding why the bin had not fallen off the door I showed it to Sister Rupert, who had disappointingly replaced Sister Emmanuel. She was not amused saying she could have had a heart attack. I had placed the bin on top of the door and there it stayed when she opened it. I learned later that I should have balanced it on the architrave as well. By then I had moved room again and discovered that Charlotte, a fairly new girl who had become my best friend and who was exactly a year and a day younger than I, walked in her sleep. Shortly after the round one night she came into our room and walked past my bed to June's compartment.

'June... June,' she called.

June slept on but I answered,

'Charlotte?'

Charlotte was just as silent as June. I got out of bed and followed her. She searched the entire house with eyes wide open looking for her room and inspected every door number. After a while I put the lights on and talked to her but she took no notice. I followed her to her bed where she climbed in unaided by her arms and slipped in under the covers without disturbing them at all, which left me baffled. I left her room only to find Sister Benedict, whose room was at the far end of our floor with my room being right next to hers, marching along the corridor demanding an explanation so I told her exactly what happened and a great fuss was made of Charlotte the following day by Sister Kevin. Sister Benedict worked in the office of the main hospital and was probably summoned to sleep in the nurses' home because of her strictness. I actually liked her but I am sure she did not like me.

Not long after that I was moved to room nine at the other end of the corridor; next to Sister Emmanuel's room. There I made friends with Victoria. She and two others shared the room with me. I had a habit of getting up every morning and dressing in silence, except when spoken to. One day Victoria and I were walking through the convent grounds where all the other nuns lived *(in the convent, not the grounds)* and she asked,

'If I tell you something, will you keep it a secret?'

'Yes, of course I will,' thinking it was about her.

Having had my assurance she told me what I had been getting up to during the night; how I acted out entering a shop,

'You said, "Ding dong," as you opened the door of the shop. Then you said to the staff, "I'm looking for a bra but I'm a size sixty and can't find one to fit me." The lady didn't have one. You came out of the door, sang, "ding, dong," and closed the door. Another night you stood on the bed and sang, "Sing Hosanna to the King of Kings," quite loudly.'

'Did I have a nice voice?' I asked, very interested by now.

'Yes. You also got out of bed, looked for your waste paper basket then opened the wardrobe door, rummaged through it and said you were looking for your dynamite.'

By then my eyes were wide with disbelief and I decided someone needed to be told after all. Victoria continued,

'You won't tell anyone, will you?'

'No,' but already knowing I would.

'What time did all this happen?'

'About three o'clock and one morning you went over to the door, switched the light on then came to sit on my bed, got up, went over to the door, opened it, looked out, closed it and switched the light off.'

I did not know if she was telling the truth but I had witnessed Charlotte and asked,

'Did I have my eyes open or closed?'

'They were open.'

I decided this was indeed serious.

'Last night you got on your bed and became very threatening. You had a knife in your hand. Tessa and I came over to your bed but you said, "If you come any closer I'll use this."'

I did not have a real knife but the behaviour was extremely disturbing for them. Victoria tried to get Sister Emmanuel up. When she did not answer she knocked a second time but when that also was not answered she decided not to bother again. Immediately, on getting up the following morning Victoria was quick to question me,

'Has anyone just been over to Tessa's compartment, or did you go over there?'

'No.'

She proceeded to inform me that I had gone over there, opened the window, looked out, closed it then got back into bed.

She reckoned I would remember as I had just woken up. A few minutes later I announced,

'What am I doing in my uniform? I'm off today.'

Thinking nothing of it I changed back into my nightdress and went back to bed. Victoria was convinced I never said good morning because I knew all about the behaviour and did it all on purpose. I relayed what Victoria told me to the nuns. I was not taken seriously and Victoria had been betrayed, but for good reason. It had not been about her but about me and naturally I became concerned and I could not understand why she told me not to mention it.

Eerie events were not common but one night when we were waiting for Sister Benedict to do the rounds I heard sharp knocking coming from the next room and, at first, thought it was somebody playing around. I went in to Patricia, another cadet in the next room and asked,

'Have you been knocking on the wall?'

'No.'

I went back to bed. She knocked again so I asked her again but she denied it. The knocking continued and so we needed to investigate further. Victoria went to ask the girls upstairs if they had been knocking but they denied it also. A full scale investigation was under way. Sister Rupert happened to come to our room. She was more tolerant than anyone else. I told her about the knocking and asked her to listen. She waited, there was silence but when she left the room the knocking continued. After doing that a few times I asked Sister Emmanuel, who was then on the scene, to stand in Patricia's room next door and Sister Rupert in ours. Again no knocking could be heard. The whole thing got out of hand. Both nuns investigated upstairs as well. No one had been knocking. The next thing I knew Sister Emmanuel brought in Holy Water and sprinkled it all over us. Everyone went to bed but the knocking continued and I was getting extremely upset about it. Eventually, Sister Benedict rushed in and commanded in her familiar Irish accent,

'Get out of bed and go outside!'

I got out of bed. She hustled me about with her hands.

'Let me get my dressing gown and slippers on,' I said half respectfully.

'I've already checked outside but you can see for yourself.' Her top lip raised slightly in her typical Irish fashion. 'I'll phone the police and they will come and take you away,' she added.

It was not my fault but I was there so as usual got into trouble as I was the only one who complained. Sister Benedict dragged a terrified Rachel downstairs but I was too smart for her. I had already planned my escape. As soon as the front door opened I ran for it across the convent drive and gardens and out onto the street. I thought about going to my brother Richard's flat a few streets away. He had recently married a nice girl called Emma; we all liked her a lot. I was also wary of strangers on the way so decided to walk slowly back across the grass and hide at the side of the convent till morning. However, when I was half way across the grass I noticed all three nuns looking for me. There was nowhere to run in that stark open space and I was convinced the police would be there. Sister Benedict had a phrase for us girls when she was not happy with us and used it then,

'You'll get the next bort horm,' as only the Irish do.

Sisters Rupert and Emmanuel repeated after her that I would get the next boat home, to which I replied,

'You know jolly well I haven't got a home.'

The next day I did escape to Richard's flat where he welcomed me warmly but the nuns came for me and that was that. How could they have possibly known I was there?

From home Richard had moved into Alan's lodgings and lived there uneasily; renting from gangster types and other dodgy characters for about six months before moving to a small house elsewhere. It was his job working in a brewery that secured it for them. Their new home was attached to a pub which they meticulously cleaned up every night for many months on their return from work. It had been occupied by drunks and needed everything thoroughly scraped from the top of the wallpaper to, and including, the floors in order to make it habitable. We girls enjoyed visiting them from time to time without Daddy's knowledge. They explained that in the winter the blankets were frozen solid on the bed and the air dripped with condensation.

Richard had not been aware that I reported Daddy but even when we all lived at home I heard him say he would write him a letter when he left. If he did, it never came to anything. It was that remark that gave me the idea of rescuing my sisters when I left.

Richard had severed contact with Daddy after he left home but was back in touch with him before he met Emma. When he introduced her to him before they were married, Daddy retorted,

'There's plenty more fish in the sea.'

It did not please Richard or Emma much. When Daddy became used to the fact that they were determined to marry he offered our old house to them as he had bought one elsewhere. He said he would advise the council and finalise that they would continue to pay the rent and live there once they were married but after Richard and Emma redecorated two rooms and painted a few doors in anticipation Daddy changed his mind, giving them no reason why. This stunned both of them and they started frantically looking for somewhere else. I am so pleased they ended up where they did.

He had met Emma at Alan's twenty first birthday celebration. He and some of his workmates got together to arrange a cask of beer for the occasion and sent out invitations to friends and acquaintances. Emma was one of those invited. She worked for the insurance broker that Alan worked for and so out of that meeting they started going out together and she became his fiancée. Their wedding took place in Hockbury at our old church, St Wilfred's. Daddy had been invited as well as us girls and he was looking after their camera. We were petrified of seeing him, being sure he would have been invited. When we arrived he was sitting at the beginning of the second row at the right hand side of the aisle where we were ushered into. We had to get past him to get to our places; Peggy, Samantha and myself. We argued frantically about who was to sit next to him. As I entered the row nervously, I accidentally knocked his books off and though I felt too terrified of lingering to pick them up I did so nevertheless. At the beginning of the service he upped and left *(with their camera)* because we girls had been invited too. Richard and Emma, therefore, could not take any photographs of their own wedding.

Emma wore a red suit; it was her preference. The wedding was disappointing but it was Richard and Emma's special day and I wanted to do my best for them. When the priest required the congregation to sing, or participate in prayers, hardly a squeak could be heard by anyone so I piped up as loudly as I could, feeling concerned that my family had not done better. Perhaps they were just shy and I certainly did not have a loud voice to make any meaningful improvements. The reception was held at their flat where I had fled to. They lived there until they disappointingly left the country but before they emigrated Peggy joined me at St Chad's Hospital. I had been to the home she was living at and told her, after we had barely said hello, that I had her uniform ready. I had to rescue her from that home as soon as she was old enough to come, not a day later. Richard and Emma visited us on occasions at Swanfold; days I cherished.

As the weeks went by the nuns introduced a teacher who volunteered to hold classes in preparation for our entrance exams into nurse training. Peggy was the classroom clown and Mrs Franklin was always sending her out of the room. We enjoyed the lessons and looked forward to them.

At meal times we ate in the hospital canteen. Bella, an older tall and thin lady was the canteen boss famous for her all in a row sneezes of twenty or more.

'Ban-an-as for breakfast girls, ban-an-as for breakfast,' she cried as we entered every morning before duty.

It was there we learned to cut up bananas to top our cornflakes. Afternoon tea was my favourite meal and something never to be missed. If we went to town we had to be back for that. Tea was jam, marmalade or syrup butties, the choice was ours. It was strange calling them butties as I thought only bacon sandwiches were called butties. We made them ourselves with what Bella laid on the tables. When the bread was fresh, tea lasted a long time. On days off we made our own breakfast in the kitchen at Swanfold.

One week all the cadets decided we had had enough of eating chunky dog food every Tuesday for dinner. We upset Mother Stephen, the Mother Superior, by going on strike for that Tuesday's meal. When nobody went down to the canteen Mother came to me,

'What's going on? Why isn't anybody going down for dinner?'

'They are on strike cos they say it's dog meat.'

She was disappointed and pointed out,

'People in the third world countries would love to have that food.'

She had worked there herself. I, being sensitive, felt it keenly and so persuaded the girls not to do it again. Shortly afterwards, because I did not want to grow any more, I gave up meat altogether. All protein, apart from milk, was stopped. Wearing 'adult' clothes still did not feel right to me at all.

Sister Kevin had introduced me to Mother Stephen because she found me difficult to handle and that introduction was the start of a lifelong friendship. The mother love I craved was right there but nuns were not affectionate or not allowed to be so I was left without. Every week I was getting into trouble and sometimes the trouble may have been exaggerated just to see her. I longed to be held like a baby but that was never to be, especially with a body my size and so I was trapped in my infantile emotions. Every evening I put a note in her place in the chapel. I worked out that she knelt where the bell was; about half way down on the left hand side. Getting it there at the right time was of the essence if I did not want to be caught so I went when they were eating supper in their refectory. My notes were full of problems and insecurities when all I really needed was to spell out my real need to be nurtured and loved like a child but never dared. After their meal they went into chapel to say Vespers, something I never attended. I worked out what time they would finish and, when I felt sure the coast was clear, I used that time to go along Chestnut Ward to the upper part of the chapel and peer down over the dark, oak balcony to see if my note had gone. It usually had and my heart filled with fear of what Mother would say or do. It was the same fear I had had of my father but she always had time to talk to me about them.

On my seventeenth birthday I was in for a real surprise. Sister Kevin handed me a present. My face lit up as I accepted her kindness but its expression dropped as I felt the shape of one of the items. It was a pair of scissors. I knew it was not a gift but a cruel joke. I had lost those scissors many months before, together with my radio and reported them both missing. The radio was with the scissors but, unlike the scissors, I could not guess what it was. At least now I had both of them back safe and sound. Devoid of any words to describe the hollow feeling on the inside of me I waited all day in case a real gift followed but it never did. Perhaps I should never have been born.

As time went by my behaviour grew worse and I became suicidal and depressed. Peggy and I fought at times and I ran off scared if I hurt her. One day I hit her hard on the head because she was teasing me and Sister Kevin sent me to Sister Benedict's office at the entrance to the hospital.

'Wait in that room,' she ordered, pointing to the opposite door.

She called for a psychiatrist who would be talking to me later. Full of fear I scanned the room and caught sight of a gas fire opposite. I tried to turn it on. If Sister Benedict came in it would have been useless. She would smell it way in advance of me dying. Perhaps I could dive through the window but we were on the ground floor so that was not much use either? I wanted my life to end. After seeing the psychiatrist, who arrived that day and was not that helpful, Sister Benedict came in and started to tell me off but I escaped through the door and ran in the dark away from her torment. She was in hot pursuit but as always I planned to shake her off. As I headed towards Swanfold's gates I about turned to where the dustbins were and banged my head against the wall till I saw stars, trying to knock myself out. The nuns caught up with me and I remember nothing more. Every upheaval to my emotions proved traumatic but who was there to create a safe haven for me?

Mother Stephen, a few days later, wanted to see me in that same room and told me there was a home that I should visit. I was not aware that it was the type of home I wanted to avoid when I left Lincrest and one that I had rescued Peggy from, so dressed in my best clothes. Mother came with me and we stayed for tea. If she had not told me I did not have to go I would have ended my life; that was for sure. The girls were swearing, smoking, shouting and I even heard that one of them had been murdered only the previous week by one of the other residents. That was not my scene at all and I could not get away fast enough. How they thought it would benefit me was beyond any reasoning so I did not reason, just flatly refused to go. I stayed at Swanfold. Mother did not influence my decision other than saying I had a choice but I felt sure that within herself she did not want me to go.

The following Christmas there was a party in Swanfold and as always a battle of wills with Sister Kevin was not missing. Father Christmas walked into the hall where the party was going on. I knew he was a nun and, even so, I never could cope with anything false and cleared off to the back of the hall. I was petrified as the red suit approached and made me its target. I quickly turned to face the wall and burst out crying. The nun in the red habit was upon me and I flew from the hall and into the next room but Sister Kevin followed swiftly behind. She came so close to me that I could barely breathe.

'Give pleasure to Mother, give pleasure to Mother.'

Meaning, 'enjoy the party'.

I could give pleasure to no-one. I swore at her. I knew she did not understand why I behaved the way I did and that nobody ever would. Sister Kevin reported me to Mother and again I got told off. She sat with me in the convent garden the following afternoon and told me quickly,

'I have only heard that kind of language coming from men working on building sites.'

I was very unhappy indeed and left her company wondering if I would ever be out of trouble.

We girls fulfilled our commitments to the Catholic faith, attending Mass as many times as it was held in the chapel, benediction every Sunday afternoon and confession on a Saturday. If we continued to do that we were okay with God from His side of things, or so we understood. We were doing what He wanted. Our tradition was upheld but that did not help my character at all, I remained me.

After two years at St Chad's some of us cadet nurses' time there was up; we were old enough to go onto our nurse training. Those of us who wanted to go on to do our State Registered or State Enrolled nurse training were helped by the nuns with applying to the various hospitals we had chosen for our future development. I applied for my State Registered Nurse training. To become qualified after a three year course would be a dream come true. Walking in my mother's footsteps was one way of identifying with her.

Chapter Eight

Nurse Training

I was glad to have stayed at St Chad's instead of that awful home and given a chance to go forward to nurse training. Most girls went to Cheshire Infirmary. A few went to Woodside Hospital a bit further away. I, however, was persuaded by a friend who lived in Flenkton, though she was hardly a close friend, to train at Flenkton General Hospital which was even further away and where she lived at home with her mother.

'Will you stay with me? I don't want to come if you're not going to be there.'

She assured me she would not leave me on my own. Believing her, off I went to my interview. The school of Nursing at the back of the hospital situated in a spacious area, with a lido to its right, looked posh and clean. It was not too big either like Cheshire Infirmary or Woodside where I would have felt threatened with so many more people to get used to.

I took an intelligence test as I had no O or A levels. My IQ was a hundred and twenty nine and sufficient to be accepted for State Registered Nurse training. I was over the moon and especially as the Senior Nursing Tutor did not have enough time to interview me properly. Next, I had to face a medical examination. Sister Benedict, when notified of the results, was furious. My haemoglobin level, being only sixty three percent, meant I was very anaemic, most likely due to my refusal to eat meat or protein to stop my growth. I think that is why, when I stood up sharply one day, hundreds of tiny sparks flew past my head, a frightening moment.

And so I left the familiar institution of St Chad's Hospital and embarked on the career of a lifetime. Because I was accepted I felt trusted; the future seemed promising. Carrying my small red suitcase I arrived at the lodge of Fareacre Hospital that September and signed myself in. The warden handed me a key to my new home; Room 5, Fareacre Nurses Home. The huge, dark grey stones making up the buildings characterised older times, possibly Roman. Flenkton and Fareacre both served Flenkton and complimented each other; caring for different categories of patient. The rooms in Fareacre nurses home were much better than those at Flenkton so I was glad not to have gone there. My room was big and well furnished. I was proud of it. I wandered over to the large window where I viewed a huge green below it and, in the distance, open countryside stretched for miles with an odd farmhouse and barn dotting the landscape. The bathroom was conveniently opposite so that was no problem, at least not at that moment. I loved the quiet atmosphere of Fareacre but could not join in with people, except on a one to one basis and that, only once.

At age seventeen I was the youngest student nurse in the class with only two weeks to go until my eighteenth birthday. I enjoyed the first few weeks in the classroom held at the training school where my interview at Flenkton General took place. The introduction classes lasted for six weeks. After that I experienced my first ward; men's medical. It was a bit of a shock to acquaint myself with a dead body for the first time. As I laid him out, with the help of an auxiliary nurse, the old man let out a breath as I rolled him towards me. I jumped back not wanting to touch him again but the auxiliary explained they all did that; it was the residual air in the lungs escaping and that he was definitely not alive.

While off duty, back in my room, unusual urges to throw myself through the window were ever present. It did not make sense when the surroundings were so beautiful. I mentioned my feelings to the personnel manageress but no help was offered. On the wards my meticulous work carried on as usual and I learned quickly. The ability to perform well compensated for the fear and lack of confidence. I did not know I was suffering from either. I was just being me getting on with what was left of my life.

I loved work on the wards and when duty was finished I did not want to go to my room. However, once there, I tried to occupy my time with study. Not only did I have my SRN assignments to do but I sent off to a correspondence college for four O level courses; geography, history, English language and maths. I got into a good routine but remained solitary. When I needed a break to go to the toilet I walked to the door and stood for half an hour straining my ears for the faintest noise. If I heard as much as a pin drop I could not venture out. Reaching for the door catch as quietly as possible, at what seemed the best moment, I turned the door knob, opened the door slightly and stopped to listen again. If I could hear any noise I quickly closed it. When the coast was absolutely clear I made my next move to cross the corridor to the bathroom. It was the same routine for the return to my room. Up to an hour of my time was wasted by the seemingly ridiculous behaviour.

On my way to and from duties, once outside my room, I dashed down the corridor at what I worked out to be a 'safe' time; a time when I was sure no other person appeared. I caught the bus from outside the hospital down one road and walked up the other of equal distance, calling into a newsagent to buy a bar of chocolate for my breakfast. I was not confident to even consider going into the canteen or make my own in the communal kitchen. The chocolate went straight into my pocket, well concealed from human eyes. I undid the wrapper slowly; not wanting to raise suspicion from passing motorists. When I felt certain no one would notice I quickly slid two thin slabs into my mouth and sucked them till they melted. I did not want to be caught chewing. By the time I reached the hospital every trace of breakfast had to have disappeared.

My second ward experience was men's surgical at Flenkton. Nurses already working on the ward described the sister in charge as a dragon; naturally a person not to get on the wrong side of. She had done nothing to harm me but I did not want to find out what she was capable of. On my way along the corridor when she was in sight and walking towards me my face flushed bright red, as though shot at by her invisible flame. With every dreadful step I veered closer to the wall so that by the time she was upon me I was so scrunched up with my face to the wall that I almost disappeared through it. When she passed I breathed again. My behaviour did not improve with time or familiarity. I am sure the habit did not go unnoticed by her. What moments I did have in her company were usually quite pleasant and not at all dragon like. What people said did not help increase any trace of confidence I may have possessed.

When visitors turned up in the afternoon it was the highlight of the patients' day and, as I was only just discovering life on the outside of our prison of a home, I wandered around the ward and got into conversation with a lady aged about forty. I asked if the older lady she was visiting was related to her.

'She's my mother.'

'Your mother?'

I stared at her. How could she have a mother at forty years old? Surely she did not need a mother after eighteen when we were no longer allowed a Child Care Officer. It took me a while to figure out that a mother was always related to a person and did not stop being a mother just because the child grew up.

Other wards I experienced were male surgical, female medical and surgical, orthopaedics, gynaecology and geriatrics. When the time came for my geriatric training I encountered something I never thought possible in the nursing career; neglect! My heart went out to those poor people. Disambulant patients had to be turned every half to one hour to prevent pressure sores but that was not always carried out. Neglect of this sort made me angry so I took the matter into my own hands. Frogmarching myself with a trolley to the needy people I dealt with it the best way I could, leaving the other nurses to talk among themselves. I was taking care of patients they had been allocated to as well as my own.

On another geriatric ward later on I got into a bit of trouble. It happened in my first year while I was in charge and the only nurse on night duty. While reading, or doing something equally energetic like knitting, I heard a heavy thud. It sounded as if it came from the ward opposite so I did not investigate. My conscience was nagging but I stayed where I was. An hour or so later a Nursing Officer arrived with her torch and inspected the ward from one end to the other. When finished she came to me with the news.

'There's a patient on the floor.'

Whoops!

'I heard a thud quite a while ago,' she said, 'did you not investigate?'

'No, it seemed the noise came from the other ward.'

'Well, you should always check. At night especially you can't always tell where a noise is coming from.'

The patient was fine but I learned more that night about responsibility than I may have done without the experience. If the lady had sustained injury I hate to imagine what the consequences would have been.

Months went by and time crept up for my first practical examination; the aseptic technique. I chose my examiner for her motherliness and was certain to faultlessly sail through the exam. I had practised and perfected it over a period of time. On the day, not used to being the centre of attention, I lost all confidence; carrying a dirty swab over the top of the sterile trolley and other things I knew not to do. Trembling, and with face and neck red, I finished the assignment but knew I had failed; at least I had not run away. Mrs Parkin later questioned me in the office as part of the verbal examination. I wondered if it was worth answering if I had failed anyway but remained calm till the end and later on was able to tell her what I had done wrong. To my surprise and relief she passed me.

I was still unable to make friends, even over the course of time. Georgette, the girl who invited me in the first place, had not kept her promise. Her betrayal surprised me so I asked my best friend, Charlotte, from Swanfold to come to train at Flenkton. She agreed but failed the interview as she had 'acted immaturely' in the waiting area.

During my troubles and loneliness I sought an answer and tried to find God. I continued to go to Mass but that was a ritual and did not address personal problems. Certain magazines offered help through reading the stars and offering potential solutions. I sent for character reading programmes, talismans, and even how to read tea leaves. These were offers in the magazines and not my searching specifically for them. I had not been taught to study the Bible or even read it. I always prayed as a good Catholic but there was no power of God in my life. Then one evening I walked into a newsagent when visiting Charlotte at Swanfold. There were books high up on one of the shelves. I noticed one entitled, 'This is Spiritualism'. Standing on tiptoes I reached up and took it down then read the words on the back. I searched its contents for the word 'God' which I found towards the back as I flicked the pages. The yellow book was safe. I took it back to Flenkton and hungrily began to read. Not wanting to put it down for too long until finished I took it the next day on duty with me and, hiding in a side ward during a period of quiet in the afternoon, I continued reading. A couple of days later a nurse walked into the side room and caught me red handed but showed an interest in it. I showed it to her and she in turn, unbeknown to me, reported me to the Nursing Officer but I had stuffed it under the mattress just in case. The Nursing Officer was also a Catholic and attended the same church as me. Opening the door of the side ward, she demanded,

'Where is the book you are reading?'

'What?'

'Show me the book.'

Reaching under the mattress I brought it out. She said nothing but would not speak to me again. If she had explained that it was wrong to be reading because of what it was about I would have stopped there and then. People jump to conclusions about others many times and that is a shame. I could have been saved from a bad mistake. How could I have known that it was wrong without somebody telling me? After all I had found the word 'God' in it so what was her problem? It was not a book a Christian should be reading, no doubt. I kept searching for answers and went down a path I thought was good. I bought a book on beginner's witchcraft that had benign practices of reading tea leaves, reading lines on the palms of the hands and such; nothing disastrous, just an explanation of life and trying to make sense of it all and to get a glimmer as to what my future might hold.

I made it half way through my training and was counting the time to my finals which were coming up in a year and a half. During my next period of training in the operating theatre I learned how to make up operation packs, lay out theatre trolleys, tie surgeons' gowns, scrub up and how to assist surgeons at operations by handing them the required instruments in the correct sequence. The time came for me to assist one surgeon performing a tonsillectomy. He asked for a wrong implement during his operation so I refused to give him anything. A stubborn stare maybe. He repeated his request a couple more times but I remained stubborn until he received the silent message and asked correctly.

After about a month in theatre I became extremely lonely, especially at weekends when no operations were being carried out and what proved later to be a stopping point for my nursing career. On days off I travelled to see my sisters at Swanfold or Sister Stephen *(who was no longer known as Mother and had left St Chad's by then)*. She was living in a small house with three other nuns in Bradhurst, Lancashire. After catching the train from Flenkton to Cheshire I caught a bus to Bradhurst and sat alone at the front, right hand side of the top deck. In spring and summer the countryside was awash with colour. I loved watching bus drivers wave to each other as they passed in opposite directions. It was the only thing that made me smile and nobody saw me do it. Smiling was still a 'sin' even though my father was well out of my life. With sadness but in the security of my little escape, I occasionally looked down through the 'periscope' onto the driver's, bald or otherwise, head. When I looked back at the trees, lush green leaves and grey tarmac road, I sang,

'Take me home, country roads, to the place I belong,' by John Denver.

I would lose myself in imagination to the fields and road ahead becoming one with them. I did not like the end of the journey as I was not safe anymore. Once at Sister Stephen's I helped clear up the front garden and, when called, went in for dinner but that became unacceptable to me. It was cold spontaneity and I needed closeness and warmth. On another visit a few weeks later she called me in for dinner and I pretended not to hear. She called and called but I did not answer. It was no use she had to come out.

'Didn't you hear me call?'

I detected a little anger; not the love I hoped for.

'No.'

I lied but she had fed a molecule of parched humanity within, albeit unwittingly. How could I confess my need to be held, to be wrapped up in pure motherly affection? It could not be done. The hunger did not relent but only grew more acute until, one day, I wrote a note and asked for what I needed and longed for. I was not expecting the response I got; an accusation of homosexuality. I became bewildered and depressed. Normal people never had to suffer that way. They had their parents and were able to bond with them naturally. In begging from strangers though, there was always the risk of being completely destroyed by their artist impression of who I was. The painting they would offer to others was bound to look like an abstract in comparison. If it was presented on canvas I would have the right to sue for a faked representation of the real me. I left that day feeling that all trust was gone.

Travelling back by train to Flenkton once I reached Cheshire, after the bus ride, was also an escape. I sat and daydreamed, staring in only one direction for the half an hour journey except when I turned my head while passing Daddy's house, part of which could be seen from Baker Boys Station. Once off the train I walked through the streets with my head down and with the aid of my thick rimmed, dark brown glasses, hid my face. I crossed the road one time to the side my bank was on and noticed an advertisement placed in the front window, 'Talk to us about your problems in confidence.' *Oh, some hope.* I could not cope alone anymore so walked inside and asked to speak to someone and in turn the manager took me into an office and listened to me for at least an hour. I admire his patience as he sympathised attentively to all my problems. I had not understood at the time that 'problems' meant financial. The bank manager did not explain either so I left innocently unawares of wasting his time but feeling thankful that somebody had taken the time to listen.

Once back in the theatre the loneliness grew until I became thoroughly depressed, though I did not know it was depression, so decided to go to the doctor. One was only supposed to see the doctor for illnesses, I thought. I did not think I was ill but he came out with,

'You are suffering from fear and anxiety.'

How could fear produce something that does not feel like fear? He prescribed drugs; I would get better! I took the drugs but even with those could not cope with the intense loneliness, an abyss of belonging absolutely nowhere and to absolutely nobody. One Saturday while working in the theatre I took an overdose of five tablets because that was all I had left of my month's supply. I had learned that from Charlotte at Swanfold who had taken one when I was still there. She was treated with love and care but when I took one a door was literally slammed in my face and I was left to get over it alone. If I had received the correct handling then I probably would never have touched another tablet. A theatre nurse found out what I had done and I was immediately sent to casualty for a stomach washout. Why such harsh treatment for only five tablets? They admitted me to the psychiatric ward at Fareacre Hospital, just a stones throw from my room. After five weeks on the ward someone from the personnel department came to see me and asked,

'Would you like to work as an auxiliary or train for SEN?'

'No, I want to carry on with my SRN.'

I had already done half my training, why do something less? I was not prepared to face the inevitable failure. It would mean a loss of even more self esteem. I gained some since I started and had achieved my aseptic technique. That was something neither an auxiliary nor an SEN needed.

'Alright, we'll give you another try.'

After a weekend out of hospital I was readmitted. I did not even make it back into the theatre. What happened over that weekend was blocked from my memory. A psychiatric nurse told me what I had done and a ward nurse informed me,

'You had been discharged for another trial period at training but at the weekend you took another massive overdose. I asked you why you had done it and you said, "Because nobody ever takes any notice of me."'

They informed Peggy who came to sort out my things and who later told me that all my belongings had been in a huge heap in the middle of the room; something that to this day I do not recall doing.

The psychiatric ward was pleasant, clean and homely and we were well looked after. I was prescribed drugs like largactil, imipramine and others I do not remember the names of. On top of those the doctor asked, through a nurse, if I would like to have electric shock treatment (*a course of eight*).

'What does that do?'

'It blocks out the short term memory.'

'You mean I won't remember what my dad did to me anymore?'

'Yes.'

That sounded like a good, quick answer. I would be able to continue with my training.

The electric shock treatments *(known as ECT)* became a highlight of the week. Every Tuesday we patients fasted breakfast because of the anaesthetic's habit of returning it afterwards. On entering the big, highly polished hall I selected my trolley, leapt on it and careered across the floor at a delightful speed. At the other end cubicles containing beds stood at the ready. The official looking anaesthetist and electrocution doctor clad in their white coats awaited my arrival. The headphone gadget lay next to the machine that packed its punch. I had never witnessed a patient receiving it, as they were always screened off. If I had I would never have allowed my body to go through those horrible, rigid convulsions I have since witnessed on television. When it was my turn I lay on the trolley and the anaesthetic was administered by injection into my arm. When I awoke my head told me I had suffered an almighty clout. Its ache pressed onto my brain like a compression clamp. Whilst in such pain I was offered a cup of hot, sweet tea by a nurse. I am not surprised. Is that not what you give a person suffering from shock? The consequences of the treatment almost cost me my best friend, Charlotte, as I accused her of never coming to see me. My short term memory had blocked out completely. She *had* been to visit me and so had others, including Sister Stephen and William who I still do not recall being there. I had understood only the bad memories of my father would be wiped out. I had been deceived. Why did they not explain all the implications, both immediate and long term, so that I could better decide against a treatment that attacked my brain rather than soothe my emotions and troubled behaviour? So now I was suffering brain damage along with all the rest of it.

Despite the ward being homely and clean it was my introduction to the mental institution which is a cold, icy, lost, lost world. My psychiatrist came round with his team once a week to inspect his patients. Before his arrival we were told to sit by our beds and wait for him. As he got closer to me my anxiety levels increased. The closer he got the more I resembled the tortoise until my head was practically submerged into my hunched shoulders. I could not speak to him at all. That kind of behaviour continued week after week until after three months on the ward 'freedom' arrived. It was sudden and unexpected. A nurse came and gave me my psychiatrist's instructions,

'Dr Carmican told me to tell you to get right away from here!'

The psychiatrist was hidden away behind bureaucracy giving me the message that I was not worth speaking to. Why could he not tell me himself that he was about to hurl me from the only home I had? Perhaps he was unwilling to face the fact that he had done me a great injustice by offering and administering ECT. There had been nothing wrong with my brain. Surely he could see that I was troubled because of my upbringing? At first the words hit like I had run into a glacier. I was stunned cold for a second then the fire of anger and the adrenalin of fear defrosted the incident at the speed of lightning. As the clash of temperatures met, a plan of immediate action exploded to the surface. I braced myself for the outburst but when it came no-one would have detected it for out of the pain of betrayal came the decisive words quietly but most definitely,

'Okay, I will!'

The shock only encouraged the existing roots of isolation to go deeper. I took another overdose but the nurse was quick in getting the tablets back up by preparing a glass of the strongest concentration of mustard. I watched as she dug a teaspoon into the fine yellow powder, put in eight measures and mix it with cold water. She then held my nose and made me swallow mouthful after mouthful until I vomited the drugs out.

That day I wrote to Uncle Len and Aunty Mo to ask if I could live with them. They replied that I could but not for three weeks. Next I wrote to Aunty Jean, who still lived in Hampshire, to see if she would have me for those three weeks and she agreed. I would not be venturing north in my yearning for Kent ever again but it was too late to be rescued as I was no longer at home with my dad and neither a child. The damage from my father was complete and the consequences were firmly binding my existence to a life of great hardship. I did not know how to live. Moving back South would prove a challenge and my expectations of a trouble free time away from home had yet to be realised.

Chapter Nine

Back Down South

My childhood training; the repetition of heartache upon heartache resulted in a character of heartache. I could only respond to life through turbulent emotions which paralysed my life. I do not recall the journey to Aunty Jean's even though it was over two hundred and fifty miles away. She had always been kind; however, I lived those three weeks in fear and dread, too scared to move. I sat on the same wooden chair every day, all day, just inside the lounge door with a book. I did go to bed at night though and responded to instructions when given them. One day she peered over my shoulder and commented,

'You've been on the same page for three days.'

I had been too frightened to read and turn over the page; neither did I remember what I read from one day to the next. She must have wondered what on earth had gone on in my life to make me behave so. But then again she may not have been at all surprised. When the three weeks were up I left Aunty Jean's disappointed with myself.

Moving back to the Bradwith's was the fifteenth move in only nineteen years of life. I endeavoured to leave all my troubles behind and start afresh. My room, the same one Peggy and I slept in as young children, was ordinary but pleasant and overlooked the average sized back garden, just like I remembered it. I set my holy pictures along the ridge near the top of the wall. They were my protection and assurance that God was with me. Settling in was difficult though and my heart was constantly racing. I did not know how stress affects the body but counted my pulse as I felt its pull on my chest. It was one hundred and thirty nine a minute so I reported it to the doctor who in turn prescribed tranquillisers and referred me to the psychiatric hospital as a day patient.

One night, a few weeks after I arrived, Aunty Mo went to bed before her husband. Just because I had been abused by my father did not mean I knew the ways of men. Uncle Len called me over to where he was seated in the lounge,

'Come and sit on my knee.' I was still an innocent child, tortured, yes, but innocent and very naive. His next words were, 'Go and turn the light off.'

I did so, suspecting nothing and sat back on his lap. To my horror he guided my hand to his private parts. The man who cared for me as an eight year old girl; I never imagined the relationship would change. That night it did. Everything in me became totally confused. Again there was no one to rescue me and I sat rigid with fear. Nothing more happened because of my lack of cooperation. I did not dare show my disapproval but I was trapped. Running from the horrors of life, the cruelty of lust and shame was to begin all over again. I would not let it continue. Stunned, I went to bed. My escape plan took seconds to prepare and the night of waiting was long. In the morning I looked at the note addressed to them both. I had written it during the night and decided it was the only solution I had. My bottle of tablets found a new home in my jacket pocket. As I headed to the psychiatric day hospital I had been attending my doom was set. I sat on my haunches outside the inpatients ward. The open door to the day room allowed a fresh breeze to penetrate the stale air inside. Feeling lonely and in deep despair I emptied half the bottle of yellow tablets into my hand and, as I had no water, it was difficult to swallow them as they were uncoated. But still, I managed to take half the contents of the bottle, twenty six in all. A few seconds later fear of going unconscious and dying shook my mind and emotions. I was only nineteen years old. Instead of going to one of the nurses in the hospital I went to the public phone box and emptied the rest of the tablets onto the floor. An irresponsible act but I did not know. I picked up the phone and called my psychologist, Geraldine. I liked her. On that occasion she was not at all sympathetic but angry at my throwing the tablets on the floor for any child or animal to consume. What else could I have done with them? Confident that they would deal with the problem I left the phone box and returned to the ward where one of the doctors asked what I had taken then called for an ambulance which took two hours to arrive. They did not seem to care very much. I did not either.

In the casualty department I lay on the trolley waiting for the usual stomach washout. A nurse wheeled another trolley set up with all kinds of medical equipment, including the familiar orange tubing, to where I lay on my left side at her request,

'Open your mouth and swallow this, it won't take long. Just relax and lie down. It will go down easier.' I tried to swallow the half inch or so diameter rubber tubing and sat up again quickly at the discomfort. 'Lie down,' she repeated. I did not sit up again but fell unconscious within seconds of her command.

Much to my disappointment I woke up at four o'clock in the afternoon of the following day with a saline drip attached to my arm by a narrow transparent tube. I watched the drips running slowly from the hanging bag. I had been unconscious for twenty six hours, one for each tablet. Nobody feels oblivion so would I ever have noticed if I had died? I had not been awake long before the duty nurse told me I had been visited,

'Your foster parents came to see you when you were unconscious,' he said coldly, 'they were not amused by your letter; they said to tell you they don't want you back.'

I was learning about dishonesty in a way that was cruel and tormenting. How can people say they did not do something when they did? It puzzled me greatly. The people I loved and trusted did not greet me back into the land of the living, nor was there anything to come back for. There was no apology for the misdeed that almost cost my life. Injustice was allowed to take its toll and I had to live out the sentence of being cut off again from all I knew. Why did I live, why, why?

I was kept on the short stay ward for a week. One side effect of the overdose was that my mouth was fixed open. The doctor transferred me to a female medical ward. My mouth was still stuck wide open as I was wheeled into the ward and my jaw ached with the strain. The entire situation was most embarrassing. The old ladies stared at me from their beds as I arrived. Perhaps they feared being swallowed up. When the woman in the bed next to me discovered I was nineteen she breathed a sigh of relief as she thought I was only thirteen and being brought to the wrong ward. The battle I had with my jaw was a long one but eventually it did close. I thought I would be stuck like that for the rest of my life.

After another week on the ward I was moved again but this time back to the familiar atmosphere of a psychiatric ward. It was to be my home for another few months. My days were spent in the occupational therapy unit where I made stools, trays and rugs. I made three stools in all. The men made the wooden frames while the female patients weaved the seats. I bought all three stools and a tray.

A particular social worker named Phil, though not on my case, was somebody I greatly admired. He took a group of us to the pub one day but I could not relate. He expressed warm affection to his clients and I felt sad that he was not my social worker. Shortly afterwards he left the hospital but before he went I asked him to sign the autograph book I bought when working at St Chad's Hospital, he wrote, 'If Jesus loves you, is he being unfaithful if he loves somebody else?' I could not understand the first bit let alone try to fathom the second bit. It was the first time Jesus was presented to me in such a personal way and sounded almost blasphemous. The second part took away the first part and I was still left out in the cold. While I was in hospital I attended adult education evening classes at the local college studying English language and literature. I finished the entire course and took the GCE exam but in the turmoil of circumstances I could not stay to wait for the results.

Whilst on the ward I met a lady named Lena who, when she got to know me, became a friend. When I was discharged and had nowhere to go, she said,

'You can come and live with us.'

I accepted her kind offer and arranged to go and collect my belongings from Uncle Len and Aunty Mo's. On arrival I found them all outside on the front doorstep. What a greeting, another stab through the heart! I gathered what little there was, put them in Lena's car and she drove me to her house. She had a husband and two young boys. They liked to watch horror films and I joined them in watching a film about dead bodies rising from their graves. Next day was Saturday and I had bought four rose bushes to put on my mother's grave. Armed with trowel and bushes I determined to plant 'Four Little Knobs' on her 'Bedpost'. It was one of the songs from that old book I found in the trunk at home and her favourite. I wanted to honour her and put a bush at each corner of her grave. About three o'clock, as I dug a hole in one corner, I gasped at the sound of a loud roar. *The zombies are rising up!* I had to get out of there double quick. My trowel could not work hard enough to dig out only two inches of soil for each set of roots. No way was I going to dig a grave any deeper. I looked up quickly as a second roar vibrated the ground and then on noticing the huge lights that overlooked the cemetery I realised it was football fans cheering their favourite team on. Trinton was playing at home. Nevertheless, I still scarpered, having succeeded in carrying out my mission.

Whilst at Lena's I took another overdose, not long after she had taken one. It worked havoc with my stomach and so I was readmitted to the hospital. Meanwhile, behind the scenes and unbeknown to me, the social services were busy trying to find a more permanent place for me to live. Miss Basebank, my social worker, found a half way house in Haxwich, Sussex about forty miles away in the countryside. So another upheaval was set before me. I came to the conclusion that the people who had 'been there' for me did not like me and I was rejected again. I needed parents, to be loved somehow. I was facing a new future, not knowing if I was to be terrified some more.

In my heart I began to relate to drug addicts and street kids in London. Perhaps that was where I should be but I knew I would not be able to communicate. When I saw posters of them, their long greasy hair seemed attractive; their pale faces looked charming but their missing teeth, not so much. At least I would have an identity but I was a decent person with morals. A new future I could not imagine. I only looked forward to the long drive with Miss Basebank. Travelling along country roads always appealed to me, especially where I could dream in isolation. I packed again to leave Kent where there was nothing to stay behind for anymore.

Chapter Ten

Apple Ash

On nearing our arrival at the new place my stomach recoiled and I frantically asked Miss Basebank if we could turn back but there was no point in doing so as I had nowhere else to go. A huge Edwardian house set in twenty five acres of land awaited us. The spooky looking building nestled quietly at the end of a long tree lined drive in Haxwich, Sussex. Green, grass verges complimenting the trees made an attractive entrance. We stopped at a small roundabout where Miss Basebank lost no time in getting out of the car and banging the huge, round, iron door knocker. Almost immediately we stood facing the housemother who looked pleasant enough with her mousy coloured hair resting on her shoulders. After a quick introduction and giving me permission to call her Karen, she gave us a tour of the house and a brief description of the daily routine. I did not want Miss Basebank to leave me there. It was winter and, after she left, the darkness of early evening shrouded any hope of escape. I was put in a double room, divided by a partition, at the far right hand side of the mansion. I chose the bed nearest the door so as not to disturb anyone if I got up during the night. A new girl who was due to come later that week would have the other part.

Apple Ash was a Catholic halfway house and after putting my things on the bed I was led downstairs to meet the other members of staff; Aunty Rose *(the cook)*, Arnold *(Karen's husband who worked down at the stables)* and Father Matthew, who wore a warm smile, lived in as the house priest. Karen and Arnold had three children; Emily aged twenty three and twins Billy and Beverly who were six months younger than me. None of their children were at home when I arrived that evening. There were seven other residents who I got to know in due course. Miss Basebank had left me to get on with adjusting to my new environment alone.

When the evening meal was ready it consisted of real home made soup, hot and brown, served in deep, shiny, black bowls, then cold meat and hot vegetables. The huge kitchen was divided into two parts but not by anything physical. The part where we sat for that first meal looked out onto a garden which I could not see in the darkness. The large pine table was covered by a busy, country patterned, plastic tablecloth. I heard Karen tell Miss Basebank earlier that the kitchen took us back to the way people lived in the nineteen thirties. Arnold was at the head of the table sitting with his back to the window. Four residents sat on a backless bench on the right hand side of the table and three sat on the left on another bench; I made up the fourth on the left, having been placed next to them at the end furthest from the window. A wooden napkin ring had been placed there by Karen. She and Aunty Rose sat at the end opposite Arnold and Karen was next to me. Wherever our individual napkin rings *(with napkins inside)* were placed by Karen that is where we sat. Behind me were two pantries and opposite was a large oak door leading to the buttery or laundry. At the other end of the kitchen, tucked to the right on the way to the hall, was another large table where Aunty Rose prepared the meals and the washing up sinks were facing it. Their stove was one I had never seen before in my life. It looked very odd with huge lids on top and doors at the front made of enamel or iron. Karen had told Miss Basebank it was an Aga. It stood opposite Aunty Rose's table. The windows next to her table and the sinks looked out onto the front drive.

I ate my soup quietly. Taking a sneaky look up now and then, because I could not ask for anything, I spied out what others were doing and how they were going about eating the meal. If nobody offered me anything I did without and my unhappiness grew. After the plates for the first course were removed, fresh fruit and cheese and biscuits were placed for people to help themselves from but I could not as too much conspicuous helping oneself to food was involved. The relief of getting away from the table was indescribable. *Let me do the washing up so I can hide my face.* Coffee and tea were served later in the library, wheeled in by Aunty Rose on a large wooden trolley.

A couple of days later when Belinda, the girl who was to share my room, arrived we quickly discovered we had something in common.

'Do you like it here? I asked after she settled in for five minutes.

'No.'

'Why don't we run away? We can go tomorrow night after supper when they are all having coffee in the library.'

'Yes, okay, I'll come with you.'

'We won't go out the front door because they'll hear us move that heavy plank across the door. We'll go out the back way and just hope we go in the right direction to find the drive.'

I felt nervous but as I had run away many times before, it was nothing new. Having Belinda for company we should be able to manage quite easily. After supper the next day I asked if she was ready.

'I'm not coming now.'

I stared at her in disbelief. The thoughts of getting away fell to my stomach. They must have hit rubber because up they bounced again high enough to reach my brain.

'Well, I'm going but don't you tell anyone I'm gone.'

'No, I won't.'

I trusted her to say nothing. After washing up I crept from the kitchen, where I had loitered until sure everyone was safely having coffee, through the long hallway and gently opened the heavy oak door into the library. Once through the door I was relieved to see the long, plum coloured curtains that stretched from floor to ceiling, were closed; they separated the games area from the television area. I had to go through the games area where my footsteps may be heard on the wooden floor by those watching the television. Scanning the library and snooker table, the sense of insecurity hammered at my nerves. *I mustn't have second thoughts now.* Like a criminal at a burglary I sneaked between the piano and the curtains, through another oak door to my left and up the steep, dark oak stairs to my room. I grabbed my black plastic coat, tied the buckled belt tight round my waist and hooked my long, black rimmed, transparent, plastic umbrella down inside the belt and left it to hang at my right side. The stairs beckoned me back down to the library. Opening the door I noticed the velvet curtains were still closed. I quickly took off back through the narrow hall which widened into the large reception area where I passed the front door. Not looking behind as I proceeded through the kitchen I pressed the lever on the door leading to the laundry, prized it upwards and yanked it open. It jarred but, being far away from the relaxing staff and residents, I feared no interruption. Pulling the door closed and finding myself in the pitch dark I fumbled for the outer door. Outside, the rain had left the ground wet. I walked up the path and round to where I thought the 'bun' *(the winter bare roundabout)* in front of the front door was. I kept walking, guessing my way. As long as I heard the crunching of gravel I was sure to be on the drive. When I reached the end of it my feet found the firm tarmac; freedom at last. I had made it to the entrance. Turning right and on up the lane I quickened my pace. Looking behind every now and then assured me nobody had followed. I was going to make it to London and become a drug addict. At the top of the lane I turned right towards houses. There was nothing but pitch dark when I turned to see the way I had come. Racing along the pavement as fast as I could, Haxwich College came into view. I had come a long way and began to relax in the assumption that Belinda had not told on me and that everyone was otherwise preoccupied with other things. Who was I anyway for them to miss? I looked behind me again,

'Oh, no!' I gasped. A car with beaming headlights was heading towards me but to my relief it passed by. 'Now what?' I asked aloud.

It had stopped in the middle of the road. Quickening my pace slightly I crossed the road to an embankment and tried to climb but it was too steep and full of briers. I ran back across the road and slipped down a crevice between the inner edge of the path and some bushes. Quickly pulling myself out I noticed Father Matthew steaming my way. Running as fast as I could I swerved to outrun him, made it past the car and continued running with all my might. He got into the car, drove very close, passed me and parked across the road, blocking my way. This time I had no room to manoeuvre but continued to run. Out he jumped, put on a sprint and whammed his arms around my body. Karen shouted from the back seat,

'Get into the car and don't you move!' Humiliated, I lost my chance of getting away. As we approached the 'bun' Karen grabbed the back of my hair tight, explaining, 'This is what we do to horses. If you grab them by the mane they *cannot* get away.' She did not let go until we were back in the library. Arnold, Aunty Rose and some of the residents were there watching a favourite television programme. 'Go and sit over by the window till this has finished,' commanded Karen. I sat diagonally from but almost opposite Karen on the wide, cushion covered ledge with my back to the window, near Arnold. He sat expressionless in his usual armchair. I knew he had been a Queen's guard at Buckingham Palace and a policeman at one time. That meant trouble for me for sure but I was so hungry for love that I forced myself to imagine him perfect and compassionate. Perhaps he would protect me from Karen? But Karen was her own boss. My stomach and nerves assured me it would not go well after the programme but when it finished Karen offered me a brandy, much to my surprise. 'It'll do you good. Tonight you will sleep in Emily's bedroom,' she ordered, perhaps because she would be able to hear me if I tried another escape. It was a room that linked the two sides of the house. Emily was away at university so the room was empty. Karen went off to get the bed ready. As I sheepishly walked into the room a little later, there was Karen facing me. Her arms extended as though to hug somebody. I glanced behind but saw no one. Silently hesitating, I concluded the hug was for me. I accepted but having not had a hug in my life before my fists were clenched behind her back and I hated the top half of her body touching me. 'Drink your brandy and tomorrow we'll start again. Forget about what has happened tonight, okay?'

Completely stunned that I had not received further punishment I went to bed but could not sleep.

Gradually, over the weeks that followed, I fell into a routine. The day started by getting up at seven thirty. Breakfast was at eight. Cleaning the sinks, bathroom and downstairs toilet on my side of the house had a soothing effect on my nerves. The smooth, gentle rubbing of enamel spoke of a problem free existence. Left alone to daydream was no burden. Coffee made by Aunty Rose for elevenses was perfect but sitting with people I still found trying. Self consciousness and blushing with inferiority had never left me. I think my redness of face must have entertained them quite a bit. The rest of the day I found things to do of my own accord. Karen soon discovered that my work was a godsend. Everything I cleaned, polished or tidied was done meticulously. That meant I was allocated or volunteered to do most things.

A few weeks after my arrival, as I lay unable to sleep one night, I paid a visit to the toilet. After washing my hands and reaching for a white towel; one of a pair hanging from the curtain rail, I noticed a car's headlights heading towards the house. It was Karen and I was sure she would care that I was not asleep. Next morning at breakfast my spirit rose a little as she began to speak,

'Who was awake last night and in the bathroom washing their hands?'

'Me,' I answered, confidently for once.

'Right then,' Karen's stern voice began, 'take those curtains down and wash them.'

'What? I thought you were *supposed* to use them as towels. You said to Miss Basebank that people used them to dry their hands with.'

As they were made of towelling, and there was no sign of any other towel, I thought it a good idea as it would save two lots of washing.

During that first summer Karen asked the residents,

'Does anybody want to do piece work at a local farm? It'll be hop twiddling and later on hop picking. You'll get paid good money for it.'

'Hops, what are they?' I asked.

'They're for making beer. Mr Merrywhistle, the farmer, will show them to you and how to do everything.' Karen explained.

She drove us down there with the packed lunches Aunty Rose had made. The gigantic field held row upon row of poles with strings tied high for the hops to climb up. Tiny, wiry hop plants protruded through the soil. The plants that were six inches or so were long enough to handle and those of us that went twiddled them round the string. They would eventually grow as high as sixteen feet. It took two hours for Beverly and I, who had been allocated the same rows, to twiddle one of the long rows and we had to be fast. It was a privilege to sit with her for lunch but I could not help comparing the lunch boxes she and I had. She enjoyed a chocolate cup cake and can of coke with hers. I had nothing special and it hurt. I was special to no one. At the end of hop twiddling Mr Merrywhistle told Karen how pleased he was with my work. I earned seventy six pounds for my first set of wages. I bought a white jacket with blue stripes down the middle of the arms and a watch. The rest I gave to Karen as I felt I had no use for it.

When the hop plants had grown and the hops were ripe the men mostly did the picking then it was all hands down sorting through them as they trundled through a conveyer belt. We had to pick out anything that was not a hop; leaves, bits of twig etc. After that we were finished on the farm then later on in the year Mr Merrywhistle invited us to go potato picking. We accepted and, being agile, I bent down to pick up between four and six potatoes at any one time, threw them into a box and by the end of the day filled fifty six boxes. As I filled more by far than the others Mr Merrywhistle asked if I would do the potato riddling as well when we finished the picking some weeks later. It was a job to be done on my own in a small outside building where potatoes 'riddled' on rollers. I selected the bad ones and threw them out.

Karen's parents, Mr and Mrs Berrygard, came to live with us after that. Mr Berrygard designed a vegetable plot on vacant ground to the right of the house and I learned a lot of gardening tips from him. One of those was,

'When you use the hose don't put it down low to just soak the soil, aim high and let the water gather oxygen on its way down. It is much better for the plants.'

Through Mr Berrygard the house became completely self sufficient. He not only worked on the vegetable plot but introduced hens also and made a large pen for them to scratch about in. Rory Strowbin, one of the newer residents, was allocated the job of looking after them. I collected the eggs for two weeks before he took over and one night, while I was in bed reading, something ran down my left cheek. I quickly put my finger on it. The next day I told Aunty Rose and she guessed instantly what it might be.

'We'll go to the chemist right away and get some head lice remover.' That afternoon I applied the solution to my hair. Immediately, my head was tingling all over. Thinking it was the solution's natural thing to do I did not bother looking straight away. When I eventually looked in the mirror I was horrified to see the front, half way down the sleeves and back of my white blouse covered with hundreds of tiny red spiders running for their lives. Leaving my bedroom in a hurry I found Aunty Rose in the kitchen. She called Rory and told him, 'There's no doubt about it, the hens have red mite,' then turning to me said, 'They're not supposed to come onto human beings but perhaps they thought you were a hen with your red hair.'

I had not noticed one mite in my hair. When there was no space left on my head one ran down the side of my face to find more room. Well, something had to tell me they were there. Rory went into the pen wearing only his swimming trunks and a bathing cap to thoroughly clean the hen house and that solved the problem.

Patches of the garden were overgrown. A particular part was dense with a crosshatch of branches and twigs. It had not been cut back for many years. With secateurs in hand I snipped away in autumn when the foliage had fallen and created a clear pathway down the side of the vegetable plot. I filled many wheelbarrows with the wood and later burnt it on the bonfire. Percy, a man who went about with Arnold, in particular enjoyed using that path. Percy lived further down the lane towards Yasling. He came round early every morning bringing huge metal churns of milk from someone's farm and to help Arnold with the horses. He also helped with the sheep shearing in summer; something I loved to watch. After that was the sheep dipping to stop tics and infections. They were not allowed to wander anywhere at those times and the sheep dog took no nonsense either. In the water they went and out of the water they came, like bullets through a shot gun barrel. I was told by Karen that an actor from a famous film lived round his area but I never caught sight of him.

Arnold and Percy trained horses for point to point races and in spring put on their red jackets to go on meets, that is, fox hunting. They gathered on horseback around the bun with about twenty hounds. Glasses of sherry were served by Karen and Aunty Rose to warm up the squad. Steam advanced in the cold from the mouths of the cavalry in preparation for the off. When ready, the Master of the hunt lifted his horn and sounded a blast of warning to any fox nearby. The sound of many hooves shifting loose gravel would unnerve any prey within earshot. Not long afterwards I watched the last hound disappear through the entrance. Sometimes I went further afield to watch but never enjoyed watching and shivering in the wintry, cold weather. I loved the sound of the hounds' barks penetrating the country air. The sight of red jackets and black hats the men wore on horseback and the sounding of the horn from a distance had a therapeutic feel about them. When the hunt was over dead foxes were brought back but I never saw what happened to them. Their absence in the surrounding countryside meant safer chickens and relief for farmers who lost much from the foxes' ravaging. I never heard of a chicken attacking a fox so was glad the vulnerable poultry were protected from being torn apart by them.

There was not a great turnover of residents at Apple Ash but when new ones came it took time to get to know them. Especially, we all knew there was something wrong with everyone who came. Some people lived there for many years. When Nathan arrived he was eighteen but looked about twelve. He was full of mischief and poor Aunty Rose got locked out of the house one day. What a tough job it was to coax Nathan to open any door! Aunty Rose was not amused and, like a mouse seeking a way into its hole, she skirted the outside of the mansion to find any open crack. Not that she was small. Her stocky build would need Nathan to open the doors wide. I felt sorry for her but at the same time Nathan was the new boss around here. I got on well with him. Shortly after he arrived I planned a cycle ride to visit my mother's grave. I had brought my bicycle with me from Trinton; the same one I bought from Mr Shabbery's store in Sunbarton.

'Nathan, do you want to come with me to see my mum's grave? It's in Trinton and will take about four hours to get there. We can spend two hours at the grave, have a picnic and then come home before dark. We haven't got any lights so we have to be back or we'll be in trouble.'

'Yeah, I'll come, okay, but what about my legs? They aren't strong.'

'Good, now you're not changing your mind and letting me down like Belinda did. Don't worry about your legs. You'll be pedalling all the time and it's not hard. Once you get into the routine they go automatically.'

Thursday came and we set off without telling anyone else where we were going, though we were not running away. If we had told them we would have been stopped. Silence was always the best key to freedom. However, we did mention that we were going out for the day. I had planned the route carefully. We cycled non stop for at least three and a half hours until reaching Harry's Hill, Stomworth; a very steep hill. There we dismounted and steered our bikes with difficulty by the handle bars with the rear wheel almost floating off the road. Everything went to plan; I laid flowers on my mother's grave so was satisfied. Our picnic refreshed us and after the much needed rest we were on our way home. Nathan's legs were fine. We had to get a move on as it was already three o'clock. About two hours into the return trip Nathan started to complain about how sore his legs were but I reassured him that we only had two hours to go and once we were home that would be that. He tried to keep up with me but as I was in a hurry to avoid the dark I put on extra speed. As darkness crept up, Nathan started to flag a little so I left him. A little while later I looked behind and noticed a policeman had stopped him in his tracks. *Oh, oh I better get going.* After the policeman left I waited for Nathan.

'What did he say?'

'He said to get off and walk and he said, "Tell the other fellow too."'

'He thought I was a boy? Oh, good.' He would never be able to recognise me. 'Well, we'll just have to scoot.' That was something new I had to teach Nathan. 'Get off, put your foot on the pedal and lean against the bike. First, though, you have to scoot with the other foot on the road to get your speed up.' It was easy downhill; we sailed freely in the windless night. Later on everything became much more of an effort the more tired we became and I wondered if we would ever get back. 'Don't tell anybody where we've been, Nathan,' I instructed as we at last put our bikes in the shed.

Next morning I was in hot trouble. Nathan told Karen and Aunty Rose everything. His legs were as bad as he said they would be but mine were fine. He promised never to come cycling with me to Trinton again.

A few weeks later I got a cleaning job in one of the local houses. It took me about ten minutes to get there by bike. The mansion stood on isolated ground and because I liked peace and quiet it suited me really well, except when I found a large walnut wardrobe with huge doors in one of the bedrooms. Noticing a tie peeping through the bottom of the doors I knew somebody was in there. It became an enemy as my imagination had its own way,

'Who's in there? You can come out. I won't tell anyone you're there.'

My hair stuck little spikes into my neck. I shivered in the spooky atmosphere. An unpleasant presence lurked in every corner. Not questioning anything or reasoning that my imagination was the problem I turned that day and left the job without telling my employer.

A new idea popped into my head. *Perhaps I should go to college?* Looking through the newspaper I found that Haxwich Adult Education College offered shorthand and touch typing courses so I enrolled and enjoyed both but did not manage to complete them, though I did learn a great deal. Practising every day with my newly bought typewriter helped me make good progress until I could not go on with the course and I left the shorthand, intending to do that later. The following year I enrolled with great confidence on a GCE Sociology course. *I could be a social worker.* Some of the other students mocked me cruelly and my school day memories flooded back into my torn life. I would not have a repeat of that history. My shell, as I took refuge in it, hid and protected me from any further onslaught. Learning politics was part of the course but it produced a paranoia that scared me silly. At night I dreamt about the Russians coming to attack me. When I told Karen she adamantly made me leave,

'You cannot go on with it. It is making you ill.'

Her overriding decision relieved me because of the bullying but I was sad to leave and not get the GCE. I wanted to help make the world a better place if successful. Not only did I fail to get that GCE but I also failed the English one I took before I arrived at Apple Ash. Despite all my efforts to improve and make up for my tragic background I was unable to make it happen.

At Apple Ash I continued to work hard. There was nothing I would not do inside or outside the house. Inside, dusting and polishing the oak banisters, doors and floors became a must. They had been neglected and become greyish in parts for want of nourishment. What an improvement when the polish was applied and rubbed up! The lively shine beamed through the house and breathing in the fresh scent of polish was enough to make me want to lie down and smell its fragrance forever. A big house like that needed a lot of attention.

Mrs Berrygard lived at first upstairs near my room with her husband. When she became unwell, after having suffered a stroke, she was moved downstairs to a room between the television room and the patio on her own. Her skin suffered pressure sores from lack of movement. My nurse training came in handy and I volunteered to take care of her alongside everything else I put my hand to.

Afternoons were mainly free up until when Mass was held just before supper. On returning from shopping one afternoon in Rockminster, a town seven miles away, I showed Karen a pair of jodhpurs I had found in a telephone box. Because they were expensive to buy, delight filled her pensive face as she reached out for them. At the same time I had a bursting headache but did not mention it. All afternoon the intense pain did not respond to any painkiller. Later, outside my room, I bent my head backwards over the banister in an effort to relieve the agony. There was slight relief but the pain continued regardless. There was something strange happening to me. I felt I could not go on for much longer so rested in my room until Mass at six o'clock. Mass was held every evening in the chapel on Karen's side of the house on the first floor, diagonal to her room. Afraid to say anything I made my way through the house and climbed the stairs to Mass. I stared a help request into Father Matthew's face but unaware of it he carried on with his preparation for Mass. After chapel I took the glass cruets that held the water and wine down to wash in the kitchen. As I walked back upstairs my energy had vastly diminished. Still unable to verbalise my predicament I placed the objects back on the altar. Having no choice I avoided going down to supper. Instead, I thought it better to go to one of the residents for help. Sandra was a good choice. I did not get on too well with her, though she was a pleasant and gentle twenty seven year old woman. She suffered from anorexia and had been at Apple Ash longer than me. She was still in her room which was one flight of stairs up from the chapel. Very slowly, I lifted one foot after the other up the steep wooden steps whilst holding onto the wall with my right hand. My body stooped a little more as I ascended each step. At the top I double turned to the right and knocked on her door with what little energy I had left.

'Sandra,' I called urgently, 'can I come in?'

She opened the door. Her pale drawn face, framed by mousy, shoulder length hair, showed its concern.

'I can't go on any more,' I muttered as I fell into her room.

She laid me on her bed. I wanted to die. My heart beat, as I counted my pulse, had plummeted to fifty six per minute. Sandra gazed at me and decided,

'I'll go and get Karen.'

Karen's attitude towards me was not a good one and I had suffered quite a bit at her hands already. I had taken it without question, simply because that is how I was always treated; with rejection and cruelty.

'No, please don't get Karen. She's good to you but not to me. Get Father Matthew instead.'

Sandra left the room. My heart filled with dread. I tried with all my might to push myself out of my body. *If only I can just get out of here.*

After a good while Karen came in wearing her outdoor clothes and wellington boots.

'What's the matter?' she stared.

'I can't walk.'

'Get Matthew.'

Sandra went and brought him to the room.

'What are these?'

He dangled his car keys in front of my face. I could have laughed.

'Keys.'

'Oh, you know what they are so it can't be kidney failure.'

Satisfied it was not kidney failure they left me and went down to eat their supper. I lay there alone trying to die but even death wanted nothing to do with me. Karen and Aunty Rose emerged later and Karen ordered,

'See if you can get back to your room.'

She stood until I obeyed. Managing to slip off the bed and onto the floor I manoeuvred myself along on my bottom. Karen and Aunty Rose walked slowly behind me, not offering any help. One by one I descended each step with a bump. I did not complain but was aware of the coldness coming from those who were meant to be my carers. Once at the bottom of the stairs they offered to help me walk to my room where I got into bed. Without discussing anything they went down to the library and enjoyed their evening. I was exhausted. Next morning I woke unable to move. With every slight movement I did make I had to rest for a long time to recover any strength. Karen came up with my breakfast. It was rare for her to show any kindness towards me so I gobbled up the small droplets of care she donated. She propped up my pillows and watched as I sat up with great difficulty. Finally, my cereal, on a tray, was placed in front of me. I was paralysed from the neck down. The spoon was already in the bowl of cereal and I had the enormous task of getting it from there into my mouth. With my elbow pressed hard against the pillow I was able to lever the spoon upwards, take a mouthful and then collapse back onto the pillow, exhausted. After about ten minutes I took the next spoonful and so on.

The chamber pot Karen brought up the night before was under the bed and I had managed to use it then and get back into bed. After breakfast, however, it took me half an hour to swing my legs out of the bed. With each movement I fell back and rested but stayed in the progress position. At nine o'clock I was on the floor not knowing how I would even get the pot out from under the bed. The battle grew intensely. About an hour later I managed to push the pot back under the bed but could not get up. No matter how hard I tried to get myself into bed I could not so sat on the floor and waited for Mr Berrygard to pass by. It was not until eleven o'clock that I heard his footsteps coming up the stairs. He rapidly tapped on the door and said quickly,

'Hi.'

'Mr Berrygard, please will you come in.' He opened the door. 'I can't get into bed.'

'I'll get Karen.'

'No, don't get Karen, get Sandra.'

He left to fetch somebody. To my dismay Karen arrived with Aunty Rose. My anxious heart pounded with fear. Both of them stood in the doorway. Karen, her hands firmly placed on her hips, demanded,

'Get into bed!'

'I can't.'

'Get into bed!' she repeated.

Without a choice I turned towards the bed. Starting to pull on the sheet I struggled to rise up. Both observers stood patiently watching. No matter how hard I pulled, my body would not respond. Ten minutes later I had pulled the sheet almost from the mattress with the effort. I heard Karen approach from behind. Next, I felt firm arms underneath my armpits. She lifted me in one movement and dumped my whole body onto the bed, at the same time shouting,

'Now, get into bed!'

Then they left me alone. As I lay there I longed in my heart for a mother to sit and talk to me, making me feel loved and cared for. Deciding to write Karen a note I managed to get a pen and paper from my locker then explained how I felt and begged, '....so please could you come and sit by me and talk to me. I really wish I had a mother just to care about me. I am so lonely up here....' or words to that effect.

Patrick, another resident, was sent up with my supper. I gave my note to him confident that Karen would understand what I asked and soon come. She did come but not to sit on my bed.

'How dare you manipulate me, making me feel guilty.'

What? I've never even heard of it. She closed the curtains and walked away. My heart, empty from longing, went numb. Next morning she decided,

'I'm getting the doctor.'

O good, I can tell him everything. Doctor Stenton arrived in my room at eleven o'clock.

'How are you?'

Karen and Aunty Rose hovered in the doorway.

'I'm exhausted!' were the only words I could say but my chance of a rescue, or at least some understanding, had been snatched away. The doctor replied,

'Well, rest then.'

I could not explain what my body was doing to me, neither could I tell what Karen was thinking but I imagined her to be feeling relieved that I said nothing to show her up. After one more day's rest Karen came up,

'Right, you are getting up today,' then waited for my response.

I struggled to get out of bed, slowly put on my dressing gown and then slippers as I could not do both at once. She watched and stayed beside me but did not help. Once out of my bedroom we walked along the landing and, like a tortoise running out of energy, I felt my way along the wall. Taking small steps and almost falling with each one I rested until strong enough to carry on. What would normally have taken me less than half a minute took twenty to get to the bathroom.

'I'll leave you now and come back later.'

I sat and waited for my muscles to perform but they were dead. No matter how I decided to pass water no muscle got the message. My abdominal muscles did not seem to be there at all. *I'll be sitting here all day.* In time, I was glad to discover the mysterious effect of sitting bolt upright and doing slow head rolls was the key to getting things moving. An hour later Karen escorted me back to my room.

'You'll be getting up tomorrow and coming downstairs.'

Not showing any sign to her outwardly my eyes widened. I could not believe what she was telling me to do. Next morning I did get dressed but not straight away. It was mid afternoon by the time I reached the kitchen. To my horror my muscles, in three days, had wasted to nothing. *How can this be?*

'You don't suit being thin.' Karen observed.

Quite early the following afternoon I was up again and, very slowly, walked to the warm and sunny patio outside where my lunch; cold meat and salad, was waiting for me on a table set for one. The others had finished their meal and I sat down to mine. Karen sat in her chair watching. I placed my knife and fork onto the meat and soon discovered I could not cut it. However hard I tried to press or push the knife and fork they floated on top like a hovercraft, just surfacing the pale, fawn coloured slice. I continued to move the knife forwards and backwards but not even a dent was made on the food. As I struggled Karen continued to watch. The usual lump arrived in my throat but my face did not register it. Karen waited for an hour before asking anyone to help me or bothering to herself.

After I recovered from that episode my usual difficulty in sleeping came to Karen's attention. I mentioned it, not expecting much of a response,

'Right, in the morning you get up at five thirty and walk around the farm.'

The farm in question was not the one Percy brought the milk from but was up the lane from Apple Ash. On reaching the lane the following morning I found the path Karen told me about and walked, clad in wellington boots, jeans and jacket. Getting round the farm took a good hour and a half. I did not wish to meet any cows as I was unsure of their character. All I knew was they were a different shape to me and much heavier. They were Friesian; I did know that; black and white. We had cows like that at Apple Ash, though I never had anything to do with them except when taking a long look at the adorable calves that were born in one of the stables. I had to do that round every morning for a week. I did love the countryside but not as a punishment and it did not solve anything.

When my daily chores were finished inside the house I helped Mr Berrygard with the garden, which I much preferred. In the vegetable patch we grew cabbages, carrots, parsnips, runner beans and other vegetables and fruit.

Percy was in charge of the meat. In spring we had fresh lamb from the field outside. I thought lambs were cute and would have loved to have been able to have some in the house. Their tightly curled coats looked cosy and to touch them I could imagine how warm they felt in winter. Percy, however, saw them and thought,

'Mint sauce.'

The food was delicious and wonderfully cooked by Aunty Rose and I often helped her prepare the vegetables. She did not seem a happy person but always in deep thought. Her cooking days continued all week. Before coming to Haxwich they had been running a restaurant in Kent. I would not tell Aunty Rose my problems but chatting to her about other things came easily. My favourite food was her flans filled with confectioner's custard and topped with fresh, succulent raspberries. The only trouble with those was that there was not a whole one each.

After dinner one day a new girl arrived named Julia who was an epileptic. I had never seen anyone having a fit before. After she had been with us for a week Karen was cleaning her room and found a drawing with the words in huge letters, 'I HATE' and became concerned.

Despite Julia's problems I made friends with her. Both her and my difficulties made a combination of rebellion, though of course, not in front of authority.

'Let's run away,' I suggested to Julia. I had a cleaning job at the pub at the top of the lane. The landlady was a good listener and heard all my stories about life and the way I had been treated. On my way back home, after finishing for the day, I said to Julia, 'I don't think I'll go now. Let's leave it.'

'Well, who's won if we do that?' she asked.

'I didn't think of that. Okay then, straight after supper.'

Perceiving Julia meant business, I trusted her. After supper, while everybody was snug in the library, the usual curtains drawn and television hiding the sounds we would make, we went out. Not the way of the kitchen but through a door in the library, across a tiny porch and out through another door. Once out of the second door we were safely on our way. Remembering Belinda, I had an uneasy feeling in the pit of my stomach about Julia but as I had been reassured by her comment, tried not to let it bother me. Nobody came to look for us. We thumbed a lift to Rockminster where Julia began to feel cold.

'Let's get some chips,' I suggested, while thinking about our sparse amount of cash. 'Where shall we go next? I think we ought to get to London.'

'Look,' said Julia pointing across the road, 'there's a police station. I'm going to hand myself in.'

Oh, not again.

'Come on, you even said to me who would have won if I didn't run away?'

She was determined though to go back to Apple Ash, so I followed.

'We'll get into serious trouble with Karen.'

'It's better than staying out in the freezing cold all night and nowhere to go.'

The police station was as good a home as any for the time being.

'Can I help you girls?' asked the policeman.

'Yeah,' said Julia nervously, 'we want to give ourselves up. We're running away from a halfway house.'

I envisioned Karen and Aunty Rose in the doorway of the police station. We answered all the constable's routine questions and the inevitable phone call to Karen was made.

'They're coming to fetch you. You are very sensible the both of you. Come on, you'll have to stay in a cell for a while till they get here.'

Sitting on the edge of a bed's bare mattress in an equally bare cell was certainly a cure for any more mischievous running away into the wild. The 'I'm in severe trouble' feeling almost lifted me off my feet. *I just want my mum; someone to hug and love me.* The ceaseless cry could not be shaken off. Though Karen belonged to her children I craved the love she showed them. When Karen and Father Matthew arrived Julia and I remained silent. We were, however, pleased-ish to see them. It meant our not having to stay the night there with the police.

'Well, at least we can sleep in a warm bed tonight,' said Julia.

In my dismay I followed her out to the car. Once home Karen's hands could not have sped to her hips quickly enough. *All I want is a hug and everything to be alright.*

'Right, you two are going to be separated from now on. I am so surprised at you, Rachel.'

I swallowed and fear gripped again as I lost what scant favour Karen had towards me and my chance of a brighter future in London. Aunty Rose stood emotionally supporting Karen as usual but where was my support? I glanced at Aunty Rose's oak like structure. There she stood as wide as the hallway and as high; the rock of rocks, the steadfast pillar and the mightiest tree. In desperation I flung my arms round her straight, sturdy body, my fingers only reaching her sides. Her cold hardness went into shock and she froze even more. It was no good. We were back no matter what.

A few days later I witnessed, for the first time, Julia having a fit. It was quite interesting and frightening at the same time. As she lay outside the chapel thrashing and convulsing, Flossy, another relatively new resident, went down for a teaspoon to put under Julia's tongue so that she would not bite or swallow it. White froth oozed from her mouth and suddenly Julia was not Julia anymore. A few days later Karen asked to talk to me. It was a surprise to be wanted by her.

'Rachel, you are Julia's friend and we have arranged for her to be taken to another home. Will you go with Father Matthew to accompany her? But don't tell her anything. Just say you are going out or something.'

I agreed to betray my friend. I felt absolutely outraged but who was I to disobey? I knew how Julia would feel but then experienced the relief that it was not happening to me. To be in Karen's good books was a great feeling and something to be cherished. Julia's possessions would be sent on to her another time. I was glad to get out of Haxwich for a day. Father Matthew drove as far as London then Julia turned to me and asked with a resigned look on her face,

'They're taking me somewhere else, aren't they?'

I did not lie and she did not make a fuss. We went on to Poppingworth where Father Matthew and I left her.

In August that year I had another experience of my body collapsing. It started as pain in my chest and the inability to exert myself. I could only do what I was asked to and not until. That Sunday afternoon Karen called for me to come to the dining room for a chat. As my strength was gone I walked in slow motion to the upright chair next to the cabinet. Karen sat at the head of the table with Father Matthew beside her and stared at me. Her interrogation began,

'If you are manipulating me, then God help you. Are you listening to me?'

Unable to answer I sat in silence. Both Karen and Father Matthew knew I could not speak without considerable effort so were prepared to wait just a little. When I did manage to answer I felt all the remaining strength drain from me.

'Yes.'

My mind was blank and all went dark. I felt that I was swimming in an abyss. Rapidly losing consciousness but, not wanting them to notice, I breathed in some deep breaths. They would have had to care for me entirely if I became unconscious and that made me feel too much of a burden. When the interview was over I went to my room without any assistance whatsoever and nothing had been achieved at all. Once back in my room I sat listening to my favourite song, 'I am a rock, I am an island and a rock feels no pain and an island never cries.' I sang in my chair for hours rocking backwards and forwards trying to get some comfort into my putrid existence. The words seeped ever deeper to find the bottom of the pain and feed it with some kind of understanding. Later, Patrick was sent up to tell me,

'Karen wants you. Come down for a drink.'

At last she cares. Because I could only respond to commands I got up and followed Patrick. In slow motion I reached the kitchen where Karen and Aunty Rose were waiting. Aunty Rose's silence always unnerved me; my shame seemed to double when she was there. The look of disapproval on her face, no doubt fed by Karen, did not need any more expression.

'There's a hot chocolate for you. And you can stop your manipulation and blackmail!' shouted Karen, then reading my plan of action, immediately added, 'And don't you *dare* throw that down the sink!'

I waited for her to finish her ranting and when she let me go I had a strong desire to get out of there again. She came up to my room the next day and was furious; thinking all I was doing was merely trying to get her attention. She loved her children and all I needed was a bit for me. I never tried to get her to love me by putting on an act. All the symptoms of my body happened of their own accord. She told me to get out of my room and go downstairs. She was further inside the room than me and I was sitting on the floor with my legs straddled so she could not kick me out. I was determined to stay put and stand up to her for once, even if sitting to do it. As she could not move me she called her son Billy who was within earshot. I liked him but he never knew. He had a girl friend called Gwen who was a lot older than him. In any case I knew nobody liked me and who would love a girl in a halfway house anyway? Billy arrived and his mother firmly directed,

'Pick her up, Bill.'

His firm arms wrapped themselves under mine and stood me on my feet. Funnily, I felt secure and protected and hoped he would stand up for me but a plan of action took over instead giving him no chance to save me. With a spurt of adrenaline I yanked myself out of his embrace and sped from the room. With my right heel I skimmed the stairs in a single movement as though on a slide. Amazed at what I had just done but too panic stricken to stop and wonder at it, I ran as fast as I could out of the house and on up to the pub. My employer opened the door to my frantic knocking.

'Please can I come in?'

'Yes, yes, what on earth is the matter?'

I told her the whole story so she hid me there for a while. Later, she spoke with Karen on the phone and I returned after being told everything was going to be alright. *How can Karen change so much all at once?*

Next day, I heard Karen shouting at Billy and then heard her exclaim,

'Bill just hit me across the face.'

I walked into the kitchen just at that moment and she repeated to me,

'Bill just hit me across the face!'

'Did he?' I asked, as though I did not hear her the first time. *It's about time somebody did.* She often kicked Nathan. One time after doing so she announced to Aunty Rose in my hearing,

'I really don't like doing that, Rose.'

When anybody told me I looked nice while wearing a certain item of clothing it made me squinch *(my own word for the face pulled after eating a lemon)* as I could not acknowledge any good in myself. At the earliest opportunity when upset with Karen or feeling acute hatred for myself I took the garment and ripped it from top to bottom. I was not supposed to look nice because I was not liked. If it attracted anybody I must destroy it at all costs.

When I paid a visit to the doctor he simply prescribed new drugs. It was the only thing he thought would help. I had no counselling, no real care, no coming to terms with anything that had happened to me and no love. Karen thought that if people thought about or did something else apart from their problems everything else would be forgotten about but this was a heart and personality issue. My entire being was broken so my mind could do nothing to fix it. Taking some of the tablets had a strange effect on me. One day at dinner I reached across the table to pick up a serving spoon and as I did so a massive electric shock surged through my body. For a brief second I lost consciousness. It was not enough to make me collapse but I felt as if my actions froze for that second, as if my arm was suspended in mid air.

'Go back to the doctor and tell him.' Karen advised.

When I did he gave me another drug to counteract the first drug's side effects. Karen did not agree with the drugs being given so freely and at her intervention the doctor stopped giving them.

The first act of generosity from Karen was totally unexpected. She took Aunty Rose out shopping to Rockminster. On her return she called me into the kitchen. There, sat on the table, was a blue metal cage and inside it a little hamster was snugly hidden away, out of sight.

'That is for you,' she said.

'For me? I can't believe it.'

Such was the shock of being given something by her. I was not ungrateful, just shocked but the reaction did not please her at all. Greatly offended, she soon let me know I did not deserve it and that perhaps she should never have bought it. I was shattered yet again by her attitude. I simply was not accustomed to anyone doing nice things for me. It was always the other way around. I took the pet upstairs and thought of a name for him, Bubbles, to match his champagne coloured coat. I was delighted. A couple of weeks later after I cleaned his cage in the buttery I carried him back upstairs. As I neared the top I lost my footing, fell onto my stomach and slid downstairs feet first. In order to try to save the hamster I hurled the cage over my head as I rapidly descended. It landed at the bottom of the stairs with a mighty crash.

Thankfully, Bubbles was not hurt in any way but I was deeply embarrassed.

Some time later Karen did something else that took me by complete surprise. She asked,

'Would you like to come out with Beverly and me?'

'Where?'

'Just for a walk.'

'Yes, please.'

I felt highly privileged. When we were ready, dressed in warm clothing and wellington boots, we set out for a wonderful afternoon. Well, at least I expected it to be good. We chatted but I felt nervous in their company. Our destination was the farm I walked through when Karen made me get up early. When we reached it Beverly went for a run. We rarely had anything to do with each other. I was a resident and she, a family member. I respected that but my impulse was to run with her into the free expanse of grass and sky. To flap my clipped wings though was a task I had no idea of doing. Karen and I talked but my heart was running with Beverly. I became moody thinking Karen would not like me to run free so I stayed with her, not only because of that, but also I did not want her to feel rejected. The mental dilemma caused me to withdraw. In the end I could not talk to Karen anymore. When Beverly came back, I knew I had lost my chance to enjoy myself and regretted it deeply. I fell into a deep silence and shut down. Karen became annoyed and decided it had not worked. If only she could have understood the newness of the situation I was again in and helped me instead of condemning my inability to adjust as quickly as she would have liked. It always took time for me to recover from those troubled situations. I abhorred them.

One sunny morning when some of us were out in the secret garden working *(a private walled area with a long, narrow pond)* we heard a sudden thud. Percy came bounding over and marched us away from the sound.

'Sandra just threw herself out of the window.'

'What?'

'Do you want a cigarette?' asked Percy

'No, thank you.'

Sandra spent some time in hospital afterwards mending from a broken jaw and arm. The shock of the incident lasted a long time for some of us. I went to visit her and asked why she did it. Her reply was,

'Don't tell Karen but Mr Berrygard abused me.'

'Did he?'

He had done the same to me once but I pretended not to notice and quickly left him but did not dare mention that to her. If Karen found out what I said, life would not be worth the confrontation to follow. While I was washing something in the laundry after Sandra came home Karen came and asked me about her father's behaviour but I pretended complete ignorance of the matter, even though Sandra said the same thing to me and more than likely to Karen. How could I make myself so vulnerable and anyway, would she believe me?

Life was not always that bad though. That summer the house needed rewiring and Mr Glayford, an electrician, came to do the job. I got on very well with him. He joked a lot and messed around. He was a breath of fresh air. During a tea break one morning, I offered,

'Here, I've bought you some sweets.'

He reached for one of the sugar coated dolly mixtures I had placed on a saucer.

'Eerrhh, eerrhh,' coughed Mr Glayford, 'What are these?'

'Hot sweets,' I explained nonchalantly.

'Right, you've had it. I'll get my own back on you.'

That night when I went to bed the light bulb was hanging from a long piece of flex almost to the ground; a pigmy lamp. Well, that was alright I could still see what I was doing. Feeling very tired I got into my night clothes and into bed but my feet reached only half way. I looked down the bed to see what on earth had happened to my sheet. They had brought the bottom end up half way and made it look like a normal top sheet. Next morning I mentioned my predicament to Aunty Rose then turned to Mr Glayford and accused him,

'You did it, didn't you?'

'Don't you know what one of those is? It's an apple pie bed.'

I tucked that one away for future use.

About the same time there was a wart on one of my fingers and I wanted to get rid of it. Another man came to the house to do some sort of job and told me,

'I can make warts disappear by absent healing.'

I had never heard of such a thing but, as I was desperate to get rid of it, I asked,

'Can you get rid of mine?'

'Of course!' he said, but frequent examination of my hands revealed an increase in wart population, in a very short space of time, to twenty five!

I learned never to trust an absent healer again. Whatever he did worked but not the way he said it would. I had to get them frozen off in the end at the hospital. I often wonder what really went on behind my back.

Occasionally, we residents had days out together. Rory arranged for us to go on a river trip one time. Clad in my pink trousers and dark green glitter jacket I was excited about going somewhere far away from Haxwich for the day.

The main body of the jacket was a plain, green velvet type material while the collars, cuffs, hems and pocket flaps had vertical, multicoloured strips of glitter with a zip-up front. I had kept it since working at St Chad's. Charlotte, Peggy and one other girl had also bought one in different colours and we often paraded around in them through the streets together.

We arrived by train about noon. Deciding to go on a boat trip first was a great idea. Sandra and I clambered up onto the roof and sat in a life ring. As boats drove up opposite we waved heartily from the top deck and for a long time enjoyed the beautiful scenery out in the open.

'Whoever is on the top of the boat please get down.' shouted one angry skipper.

'What are we doing wrong?'

No one else had been harsh like that.

'Better get down,' said Sandra.

'Why, we like it up here and we can see everything much better?'

Still, even though I did not understand, we forsook our desires to stay in the rings and went inside. After the boat trip we settled at a table for our picnic, eating heartily and healthily on chicken drumsticks, rice salad and cheese scones Aunty Rose had made, after which we were off to do some shopping. Rory gave me five pounds. I bought him a gift with it and handed it to him outside not expecting the thank you I got,

'How would you like it if you gave somebody some money to have a nice time with and they bought *you* something with it?'

The rebuke came with such force my hair stood on end. I learned my lesson fast; never again. *I'll keep it all to myself.* We had a wonderful day, apart from that, and returned to Apple Ash the better for it. Paddles, the friendly dog, greeted us with her heavy rope of a tail wagging with all its might and Silver, the tabby cat, dashed out as we opened the kitchen door. Apple Ash had two cats and two dogs, besides the horses, cows, sheep and hens.

Later that summer Samantha and Peggy came down to stay for a two weeks holiday. Samantha played her guitar and we sang folk hymns including, 'On this House Your Blessing Lord.' How I longed for that. Both she and Peggy loved the new black Labrador puppies that Paddles had given birth to. They were kept in one of the stables. I looked so much forward to my sisters' visits. After I saw them off when it was time to say goodbye my duties at the house resumed.

In May the following year Mrs Berrygard died and was laid out in the chapel upstairs. Karen took photographs of her body lying in the coffin but when they were developed not one of them turned out. When that happens, you know something spooky is going on. We were highly suspicious. After the funeral Mr Berrygard prepared cucumber sandwiches for the wake. He sliced the frozen bread wafer thin so that when it was lifted from the loaf we could see right through it and equally thin he cut the cucumber. They were the most delicious, refreshing sandwiches I had ever tasted.

My grandfather died around the same time as Mrs Berrygard. It was a very sad time because I was never free to go to places I wanted to visit very much and that included his funeral. Being on social security benefits was hardly enough to get a life with.

Eventually, Karen felt I should get another job locally as I had left the pub and had not worked for a while. I found one at a beautiful mansion round the corner at the top of the lane. My new employer was a lovely, friendly woman. Her two year old daughter was the best you could want. I loved her. Her mother was sometimes too busy to attend to her cries but I was able to encourage her to spend time with her to avoid the suffering I was experiencing. It pleased me to be able to do that much good. My work was quite hard. There was a lot of brass cleaning to be done and that made my hands black with tarnish. I would have preferred to live there than at Apple Ash.

Some time during the third year of my stay at Apple Ash Karen suffered a severe depression. Her face was taut and red. Father Matthew took her abroad for three weeks but when they came home she was no better. I took great note of this and when I left for bed that evening I got on my knees and prayed,

'God, please will You heal Karen. She has this whole house to look after, not just me. I am not being selfish. Look, I tell you what, You come with me, I'll show You the way to her room.' In my imagination I took Jesus' hand, led Him out of my room and said, 'Tell you what; I'll take you through the short way; in here.' Still only in my imagination I led Him across the landing and through Emily's room; knowing nobody was in there. I walked with Him, making sure He would not get lost or out of my sight, through the vast room and towards the far door. Not letting go of Him I took Him past the chapel, diagonally across the landing and to Karen's room. Opening her door quietly I led Him to her bedside. 'Now,' I instructed, 'Just lay your hand on her forehead and take that headache and depression away.' When He had finished I took His hand, again in my imagination, and led Him step by step back to my room as I thought He would not know the way. 'Thank You, we'll see how she is in the morning.'

And so, with antennas raised as I went into the kitchen for breakfast, I heard Karen declaring,

'Do you know, Rose, I feel better this morning.'

I kept my peace, turned my head and offered a quick smile to Jesus.

After the death of my grandfather Samantha came down without Peggy for another holiday. Just prior to her visit I had been trying to read some Christian books and other literature. I picked up a woman's magazine and read it quite easily but the Christian books caused my eyes to blur. I became a little suspicious. Something was trying to stop me from reading anything to do with God. I had been to church all my life as a Catholic but this was an unusual phenomenon. I told Samantha,

'Every time I read an ordinary magazine I can read it clearly but when I read a Christian book it all goes blurred.' Samantha replied confidently,

'It's the Devil.'

'I never thought of that.'

I knew there was a Christian Bookshop in Rombourne, Kent, so we decided to go there. I said to God,

'Well, now I know what it is I can do something about it. Please, when I get to the shop will You show me a book that will help me?'

On entering, one book stood out as though it filled the entire shop. It had a yellow cover with red lettering for the title. I took hold of it, read what was written on the back and knew instantly it was the right one so bought it there and then. Travelling back to Haxwich on the train, apart from us throwing chips through our open window into the opposite train, I read the book. So hungry was I to get the help I needed that I practically finished the entire book before the end of the journey. As soon as I could I went into the chapel and commenced what I felt I should do to have a changed life,

'Dear God, I confess all my sins and ask you to forgive me. You can have my life, I don't want it.'

I then got up and walked out of the chapel alone having left my life there for Him to get on with; not with Him to my knowledge. My life went in one direction with God, I went in another. That was that, it was done. A couple of days later I was kneeling by my bed, after Samantha had gone home, and started reading the Bible. As I read down a certain page my eyes fixed and fastened on one word. They would not move one way or the other. The word was, 'Jesus'. As my eyes were stuck fast to that word something else started to happen. It was feeling, I suppose, a bit like a continuous sunbeam pouring into me but I did not see any light. I did not understand what was happening and became scared, so asked,

'Please can you stop? You are frightening me.' It stopped immediately and then I added very quickly, 'But You can come back again.'

Suddenly, I felt very much alone. *What have I done?* He did not come back. However, I woke next morning feeling wonderful. At breakfast, Arnold observed,

'You look happy with yourself today.'

'I am.'

I had never in my life felt such happiness. Confidence oozed out of my body and soul like water, living water. Later that day I was at Mr Merrywhistle's farm telling the other workers I had no fear anymore. Even Karen asked me to sit next to her on the sofa to watch television that evening. She had never done that before. It did not even matter that she had asked me. Normally I would have been over the moon for that to happen but not then. For one week I was Miss Heaven; walking on air and as free as a bird. Then heaviness started to descend. Negative thoughts about my experience invaded my mind and I lost all I had gained except the memory of that amazing encounter. As I read the Bible I suddenly hated it. My behaviour became a nightmare. Together with my Bible I took all my other books and approached the bonfire. As I lit it and watched the fire burn, a feeling of sinister pleasure crept up inside my belly. *That's odd, why am I so happy about that? Okay, I'll just have to get another then.* I bought another Bible from Rockminster Christian bookshop. It was not long before I tore and burned that one to cinders as well and on it went until I eventually grew out of it. Before long, I started attending a non Catholic church in Rockminster. During the first service the pastor prayed for me while laying his hands on my head. Nothing, to my knowledge, happened but I felt it was the right thing to do. I told Karen and expected an encouraging word but instead,

'I forbid you to go to that church again.'

That was it then. No more church. I was mortified about her attitude. I had been attending the local Catholic Church but Jesus did not seem to be there and I felt sorry for Him. He did not seem to be at Apple Ash very much either.

The next time Samantha visited she wanted to come and work at a care home in Boreford; a village to the west of Haxwich, but after her interview she was not accepted and so returned home. Some time later, I applied to work in a bank in Rockminster but was also turned down so I sought another full time job in Chingles china and glass shop, also in Rockminster. I was accepted by the ugly but kind looking woman who sat beside me in the office. When I broke the news to my employer she told me,
'I knew that would come one day. I am so sorry to see you leave.'
I was equally sad to be going from her.
My new job was interesting enough, never boring, even though there was lots of dusting to do. I cycled the seven miles every morning and when it was raining wore my bright yellow Sowester and matching hat. Beverly said I looked like a puffin wearing those. I took her remark as a compliment. In the shop I learned how to handle 'fragile' china and glass and that you can treat it like anything else. As it is made of bone it has a strength that ordinary earthenware does not possess. After six months of working there I received a letter from Samantha to say she was moving down south to start her State Registered Nurse training at Ribford Hospital and would I like to live with her in Ribford; an ideal escape from Apple Ash? I lost no time in applying for a transfer to Chingles of Ribford. There were branches in many areas of the country. They did not have a vacancy but there was one in the Cantrin branch not too far from there. After thinking about it and being assured I could eventually be transferred to Ribford as soon as a place became available, I accepted. Samantha found a bedsit for us to share and meanwhile Peggy entered the convent to become a nun. I broke the news to Karen and handed in my notice at Chingles.
The evening before my last day at work I packed up my things and left them at Apple Ash. At five thirty after work Father Matthew came to collect me in his little blue van together with all my belongings. Once inside the car we started our journey to Ribford, I asked with much apprehension,

'Is Karen coming with us?'

'No.'

As he was driving through Twing, a village only two miles east of Haxwich, I anxiously begged him to let me go and say goodbye to Karen. A feeling of complete oblivion, deep shock and betrayal overwhelmed me that even on my last day at Apple Ash she could not take me to my new home or even say goodbye. After driving with the headlights illuminating trees, bushes, rabbits sitting along the verges of the otherwise dark lanes and the well lit streets of Sussex we arrived at the small flat to be welcomed by my smiling sister at around seven o'clock. Father Matthew helped carry my things past the pay telephone in the hall and up the stairs. The semi-detached house had three bedsits on the first floor. Samantha had secured the back bedsit which consisted of two rooms; a well furnished twin bedroom and a small kitchen cum dining with television lounge area. Just off the landing were the bathroom, a separate toilet, one of the other bedsits further along the landing and another at the front of the house. After leaving my things on the floor in the bedroom, which overlooked the long back garden with a shed at the end, though I could not see it in the dark, Father Matthew took Samantha and I to a restaurant in Ribford for a quiet meal, dropped us back home and his only word on leaving was,

'Goodbye.'

Afterward

Life outside care began with a member of my family. Something I could never have envisaged and it all happened after I threw my life at Jesus. In our new home together success was sure to follow. Samantha would never be far away because the hospital where she worked was only across the road and my new life with Jesus, albeit misunderstood by me, was about to begin.

I and my sisters felt terrible about what had happened in our lives. We did not realize that it is not a matter of just walking away unscathed from the type of environment we had been brought up in. The aftermath of such awful lives severely affects the way people function. From then on Samantha and I were on our own but the journey that lay ahead, especially for me, is recorded in my second book. I hope you have enjoyed reading my autobiography so far and not only enjoyed but learned something of what happens to children without a secure, loving foundation on which to build a more fruitful existence.

In book two I write about my experiences in trying to find a way out of the aftermath of all the brutal suffering and discovering the often hidden real reasons behind it. There were many blockages to my total freedom caused by misunderstandings, misjudgments and the devil's fightback for my soul. You will read about steps forward and backward and may find the answers I have discovered for myself could be a possible solution to your own problems. Nothing, absolutely nothing is impossible with God.

See you in book two.

Acknowledgements

I wish to express my thanks to:

Samantha - for being at the end of the phone during the process of writing this book.

Peggy - who unwittingly pushed me in getting a move on with this work. She had started to write her own autobiography and that was the trigger I needed to finish mine.

Emma Pallitan - my sister-in-law for reading one of the drafts.

Susan Hill – for her help preparing the final stages of the publication of this book.

Anyone else who has offered to help and encourage me along the way.

Front and back image of little girl: www.123rf.com.
Back image of lane: My own.